D1496158

ENCYCLOPEDIA OF ISLAMIC DOCTRINE

VOLUME 6
FORGOTTEN ASPECTS OF ISLAMIC WORSHIP: PART ONE

SHAYKH MUHAMMAD HISHAM KABBANI

AS-SUNNA FOUNDATION OF AMERICA

As-Sunna Foundation of America
© 1998, 2nd edition, Shaykh Muhammad Hisham Kabbani

Edited by Gabriel F. Haddad, Ph.D. (Columbia), Alexandra
Bain, Ph.D. (Victoria), Karim K. Tourk, Jennifer McLennan

Library of Congress Cataloging in Publication Data

Kabbani, Shaykh Muhammad Hisham.
Encyclopedia of Islamic Doctrine Vol. 6. Forgotten Aspects of
Islamic Worship: Part One
[Arabic title: *al-Musuat al-islami aqida ahl al-sunnah wa al-
jamaat*]
p.   cm.
    Indices.
Islam—doctrines. 2. Heretics, Muslim. 3. Wahhabiyah.
I. Kabbani, Shaykh Muhammad Hisham. II. Title.

ISBN: 1-871031-87-7

Published by
As-Sunna Foundation of America Publications
607A W. Dana St.
Mountain View, CA 94041
e-mail: asfa@sunnah.org
www: http://sunnah.org

Distributed by
KAZI Publications
3023 W. Belmont Avenue
Chicago, IL 60618
Tel: 773-267-7001; Fax: 773-267-7002
e-mail: kazibooks@kazi.org
www: http://www.kazi.org

CONTENTS

1. THE SUFFICIENCY OF BEARING WITNESS (*KALIMAT AL-SHAHADA*)

1.1. INTRODUCTION

Questions addressed in this chapter include:

What is the position of the mainstream scholars with regard to the aspiring Muslim's uttering the phrase of bearing witness (*kalimat al-shahada*)?

Is it better to delay the aspiring Muslim's saying of the *kalimat al-shahada* ("*La ilaha illallah* (there is no god but Allah)" on the grounds that, as some claim, it is null and void, or at best insufficient and incomplete, unless one first understands its meaning and implications?

Is there any evidence in the Quran and hadith suggesting that someone who only utters the *kalimat al-shahada* ("*La ilaha illallah* (there is no god but Allah)" enters paradise? What is the authenticity of the hadith of the Prophet's request to Abu Talib to pronounce it on his death-bed?

1.2. FORTY HADITH ON "WHOEVER SAYS *LA ILAHA ILLALLAH* ENTERS PARADISE"

It is the obligation of all Muslims to make things easy in matters of religion, and not to turn away those whom Allah causes to knock at the door of Islam in search of the path to salvation. Allah said that He did not create the *jinn* and humankind except to worship Him, and Ibn Abbas explained that "worship," in this context, meant knowing Allah. In Allah's sight, the beginning, middle, and end of knowledge is to know that there is no god except Him; He said, *"Know that there is no god but Allah"* (47:19). Therefore, any non-Muslim in whom Allah has placed the desire to say the *kalimat al-shahada or tayyiba* must be encouraged to say it on the spot and without further delay. In regard to its perfect understanding, even several lifetimes might not suffice to attain it nor have any of the Imams of the Sharia suggested anyone's Islam should rely upon such an understanding. This is because true understanding of *tawhid*, or oneness of Allah, is not a realm of actions, but of belief, and it lies hidden in the heart.

The approach whereby non-Muslims are made to linger outside Islam and ordered to read and study before they can say *shahada* is not condoned, for no one knows who will live to see the next second. The Prophet said, "Your breaths are counted."

As mentioned above, understanding the meanings and implications of saying the *shahada* comes later, as it does even for older or born Muslims. Those who seek to understand the *shahada* before it is pronounced want to see a tree bearing fruit even before they plant the seed. Allah said:

> Do you not see how Allah gave as the parable of a good word (the kalima tayyiba) a good tree that is firmly rooted and its branches reach the sky. It bears fruit at all times, under orders from its Lord. So does Allah explain parables for men that they may take heed (14:24-25).

Thus the utterance of la *ilaha illallah* is the seed, the tree, and the fruit all at once, depending on the circumstances of its being said.

Moreover, it is established in countless hadith that the mere utterance of the *shahada* carries immense blessing; namely, the Prophet's promise that he who utters such a tremendous phrase shall enter Paradise. The following is a collection of forty authentic hadiths on this topic with the Arabic wording of some of them:

1 The Prophet (ﷺ) said, "Whoever says: there is no god but Allah enters paradise."[1]

2 The Prophet (ﷺ) said, "Whoever says there is no god but Allah enters paradise even if he commits adultery and even if he steals (i.e. even if he commits great sins)."[2]

3 The Prophet (ﷺ) said, "Whoever witnesses that there is no god but Allah and that Muhammad is Allah's Messenger, Allah forbids the fire from touching him."[3]

Ibn Hajar says that the hadith saying "Allah forbids the fire from touching him" are even more explicit than those saying "Allah will enter him into paradise" in establishing that the person who proclaims Allah's oneness is saved, even if he does not heed the orders and the prohibitions.[4]

4 The Companions were talking about Malik ibn Dukhshum, and they wished that the Prophet (ﷺ) would curse him so that he should die or meet some calamity. The Prophet (ﷺ) said, "Does Malik ibn Dukhshum not bear witness to the fact that there is no god but Allah and that I am the Messenger of Allah?" They said, "Yes, he no doubt says this but it is not in his heart." The Prophet (ﷺ) replied, "No-one ever witnesses that there is no god but Allah and that I am Allah's Messenger and then enters the fire nor is consumed by it."[5] Anas said, "This hadith impressed me so much that I ordered my son to write it down and he did."

5 The Prophet (ﷺ) said that Allah will save the man in his community whose record of sins fills 99 books, each book extending as far as the eye can see. Against all this will be weighed the one good deed he has done, which is his witnessing that there is no god but Allah and that Muhammad is His Messenger, and it will outweigh all the rest. The Prophet (ﷺ) then said, "Nothing is of any weight compared with Allah's Name."[6]

These are among the hadith whose meanings have been

---

1 Tabarani narrated it from Abu Dharr in the *Kabir* (7:55), Ibn Hibban in his *Sahih* (31), al-Hakim in his *Mustadrak* (4:251), al-Mundhiri in *al-Targhib* (2:422), al-Haythami in *Majma al-zawaid* (1:18), Ibn Adi (7:2639), Abu Nuaym in the *Hilya* (7:174), and al-Bazzar from Umar.

2 Nasai, Tabarani and others from Abu al-Darda–*sahih*.

3 Narrated by Bukhari and Muslim from Ubada ibn al-Samit.

4 Ibn Hajar, *Fath al-bari*, book of *riqaq* ch. 14 (1989 ed. 11:324).

5 Muslim narrates it.

6 The hadith begins: *innallaha sayukhallisu rajulan min ummati*. Narrated from

misinterpreted by some in the present day as the Mutazila did in the past with the hadith of intercession, because these hadith do not fit their views. Those who would manipulate the very words of the Prophet (ﷺ) assert, for example, that whoever "only" witnesses to Allah's oneness is still not safe from the Fire until he meets their added conditions:

> • He must first fully understand the meaning of the *kalima tayyiba* (!);
> • His actions, both inward and outward, must first verifiably fulfill all the demands of the *kalima tayyiba* (!).

An example of the erroneous views propagated by the "Salafis" is Abd al-Rahman ibn Hasan ibn Muhammad ibn Abd al-Wahhab's commentary on his grandfather's *Kitab al-tawhid*.[7] This is a notorious reference book of the "Salafis;" a kind of anthology of errors. In the following excerpts, we see how the "Salafis" distort the reading of these foundational hadith about the sufficiency of the *kalima tayyiba* in an effort to make them mean the opposite of what is explicitly said. They interpolate the condition that one must necessarily act, and, contrary to what the Prophet (ﷺ) said, that saying the *kalima tayyiba* is not enough for one to enter paradise! This is entirely untrue and against what the Prophet (ﷺ) said regarding this matter as documented above. The Prophet (ﷺ) also said, "Whoever lies about me (i.e. about what I said) intentionally, let him prepare himself for the fire."

In the excerpt, the author purports to address the hadith of the Prophet (ﷺ):

> Whoever witnesses that there is no god but Allah alone, without partner, and that Muhammad is His servant and messenger, and that Jesus is Allah's servant and His messenger and His word (i.e. His direct order), which He cast upon Mary and a spirit which came from Him, and that the paradise is real, and the fire is real: Allah will enter him into paradise regardless of his deeds.[8]

Abd Allah ibn Amr ibn al-As by Ahmad, Tirmidhi (*Iman* 17, *hasan gharib*), al-Hakim, and Bayhaqi in *Shuab al-iman*.

7 Abd al-Wahhab, *Fath al-majid sharh kitab al-tawhid* (7th ed. Muhammad al-Fiqqi, 1377/1957),

8 The hadith is taken from Bukhari and Muslim from Ubada ibn al-Samit.

1.3. Contrary to the Hadith of the Prophet (ﷺ) "Salafis" Disqualify Those Who Only Say *Shahada*

Abd al-Rahman ibn Hasan ibn Muhammad ibn Abd al-Wahhab comments in his *Fath al-majid sharh kitab al-tawhid*:

> The Prophet's words, "Whoever witnesses that there is no god but Allah alone" refer to whoever utters them in full knowledge of their meaning and in active compliance with their demand, both inwardly and outwardly. For it is a must, in the two witnessings, to have knowledge, certainty, and actions on the basis of what they refer to, as Allah said, *"Know then that there is no god except Allah"* (47:19) and *"Except they who witness to the truth in full knowledge"* (43:86). As for he who utters "There is no god but Allah alone" without knowing what it means, nor being certain, nor acting in compliance with its demand, such as repudiating *shirk* and purifying one's words– both those of the tongue and those of the heart–and one's deeds–both those of the heart and those of the organs–such a witnessing is useless by consensus.[9]

1.4. Elaboration of the Mainstream Islamic Position on the Sufficiency of Saying the *Shahada*

The evidence is clear. The Prophet (ﷺ) included in his hadith, "Whoever says," "whoever witnesses," and "whoever accepts." He did not say, as the above writer asserts, "Whoever utters [the *kalima*] in full knowledge of their meaning and in active compliance with their demand, both inwardly and outwardly."

This is not to say that full knowledge and compliance are not necessary or meritorious. However, they are not part of the Prophet's statement, nor are they inferred by the Prophet's statement, as confirmed by other hadith that stress that the non-compliance of great sinners will not cause their entry into

---

9 Abd al-Rahman ibn Hasan ibn Muhammad ibn Abd al-Wahhab, *Fath al-majid sharh kitab al-tawhid*, 7th ed., ed. Muhammad al-Fiqi (Cairo: Maktabat al-sunna al-muhammadiyya, 1377/1957) p. 35.

Paradise to be forfeit. One strong proof of this is that the Prophet (ﷺ) was content to ask that his uncle Abu Talib merely utter the *shahada* on his death-bed, without adding any condition.[10] That is what Abu Bakr reported when he said:

> I asked Allah's Messenger what basic thing was necessary for salvation and he replied, "Whoever accepts the Word that I brought and that I offered to my uncle Abu Talib and that he rejected; this Word constitutes salvation for him."[11]

The point that the Prophet (ﷺ) makes in these paramount hadith, which is rejected by "Salafis," is that the utterance of the *kalima tayyiba* is sufficient for one to enter paradise. The intention of the "Salafis" is to dismiss what the Prophet (ﷺ) explicitly stated and declare that anyone who utters the *kalima tayyiba* is still a disbeliever. This aberration is the cornerstone of the "Salafi" heresy. The scholars of mainstream Islam have warned about this even before the time of Jamal Effendi al-Zahawi who said, "May Allah the Exalted fight the Wahhabis, because they are intent on establishing reasons to declare Muslims disbelievers. They have shown that *takfir* (declaring Muslims to be disbelievers) is their highest ambition."[12]

The following is further evidence that Allah has allowed that, for his salvation, a person need utter but once in life the *kalima* (phrase) of *shahada* (witnessing) that "There is no god but Allah alone," which is *la ilaha illallah* in Arabic. It is important to reiterate this point of belief often, as modern day extremist sects such as those who call themselves the "Salafis" deny the sufficiency of the *kalima tayyiba*, add various conditions to it, and refuse to encourage its utterance by potential Muslims although the Prophet (ﷺ) clearly stated that its utterance was sufficient for one to enter paradise.

In the well-known hadith of the great intercession, Allah four times tells His Prophet (ﷺ), "Ask and you shall receive, intercede and you shall have intercession."[13] The Prophet (ﷺ) intercedes and his intercession is accepted when all other

---

10 See below #10-11, 40.

11 It is narrated by Ahmad, Tabarani in *al-Awsat*, Abu Yala, and al-Bazzar.

12 Jamal Effendi al-Zahawi, at the end of his denunciation of the Wahhabi heresy entitled *al-Fajr al-sadiq*.

13 Related from Abu Hurayra in the last book (*Tawhid*) of *Sahih al-Bukhari*.

prophets are powerless to intercede. His intercession is accepted in four successive instances:

- For those who have a grain of faith in their heart
- For those who have a mustard-seed of faith in their heart
- For those who have less than that of faith in their heart
- For anyone who ever said, *"la ilaha illallah"*

Allah swears to this last part. This is conclusive evidence that to say *la ilaha illallah* with not even a mustard-seed of faith in the heart will earn the speaker the Prophet's intercession and salvation from the fire.

6 Mabad ibn Hilal al-Anazi relates: Some of us from Basra gathered and went to Anas bin Malik in company with Thabit al-Bunani so that he might ask Anas about the Hadith of Intercession on our behalf. Anas was in his palace, and our arrival coincided with his late morning (*duha*) prayer. We asked permission to enter and he admitted us, sitting on his bed. We said to Thabit, "Do not ask him about anything else first but the Hadith of Intercession." He said, "O Abu Hamza! Here are your brethren from Basra coming to ask you about the Hadith of Intercession." Anas then said:

> The Prophet (ﷺ) talked to us saying, "On the Day of Resurrection the people will surge one group after another like waves, and then they will come to Adam and say, 'Please intercede for us with your Lord.' He will say, 'I am not fit for this. You should go to Abraham (ﷺ) as he is the Intimate Friend (*khalil*) of the Beneficent.' They will go to Abraham (ﷺ) and he will say, 'I am not fit for this, but you should go to Moses (ﷺ) as he is the one to whom Allah spoke directly.' So they will go to Moses and he will say, 'I am not fit for this, but you should go to Jesus (ﷺ) as he is a soul created (directly) by Allah, and His Word (Be!).' They will go to Jesus (ﷺ) and he will say, 'I am not fit for this, but you should go to Muhammad (ﷺ).'
> "They will come to me and I will say, 'I can do it.' Then I will ask for my Lord's permission and it will be given; then He will inspire me to praise Him with

such praise as I cannot fathom. So I will praise Him with those praises and will fall down prostrate before Him. Then it will be said, 'O Muhammad, raise your head and speak, for you will be heard; ask, for you will be granted your request; intercede, for your intercession will be accepted.' I will say, 'O Lord, my Community! My Community!' And then it will be said, 'Go and take out of the fire all those who have in their hearts faith the weight of a barley grain.'

"I will go and do so and return to praise Him with the same praises, and fall down prostrate before Him. Then it will be said, 'O Muhammad, raise your head and speak, for you will be heard; ask, for you will be granted your request; intercede, for your intercession will be accepted.' I will say, 'O Lord, my Community! My Community!' And then it will be said, 'Go and take out of the fire all those who have in their hearts faith the like of a small ant or a mustard-seed.'

"I will go and do so and return to praise Him with the same praises, and fall down prostrate before Him. Then it will be said, 'O Muhammad, raise your head and speak, for you will be heard; ask, for you will be granted your request; intercede, for your intercession will be accepted.' I will say, 'O Lord, my Community! My Community!' And then it will be said, 'Go and take out of the fire all those who have in their hearts the smallest iota of faith.' I will go and do so."

When we left Anas, I said to some of my companions, "Let us pass by al-Hasan (al-Basri) who is hiding himself in the house of Abu Khalifa and request him to recount to us what Anas ibn Malik has just told us." So we went to him and we greeted him and he admitted us. We said to him, "O Abu Said! We came to you from your brother Anas ibn Malik and he related to us a hadith about the intercession the like of which I have never heard." He said, "What is that?" We told him of the hadith and at the end we said, "He stopped at this point." He said, "What then?" We said, "He did not add anything after that." He said, "Anas related the hadith to me twenty years ago when he was a young fellow. I don't know whether he forgot or if he did not like to let you depend overly on what he might have said." We said, "O Abu Said! Do tell us." He smiled and said, "The human being was created hasty. I only mentioned it because I was going to inform you of it. Anas told me the same as he told you and said that the Prophet (ﷺ) added: "I will then return for a fourth time and praise Him similarly and prostrate before Him the same as before. And then it will be said, 'O Muhammad, raise your head and speak, for you will be heard; ask, for your will be granted your request; intercede, for you intercession will be accepted.' I will then say, 'O Lord, allow me to intercede for whoever said, "La ilaha illallah." Then Allah will say:

By My Power,
By My Majesty,
By My Supremacy,
And by My Greatness,
I shall take out of the fire anyone who ever said, "La ilaha illallah."[14]

7 This is confirmed by another well-known hadith whereby the Prophet (ﷺ) said, "My intercession is for those people of my Community who commit major sins."[15]

8 a) *Adhana fi al-nasi anna man shahida an la ilaha illallah wahdahu la sharika lahu mukhlisan dakhala al-janna* (it was proclaimed among the people that whoever witnesses that there is no god except Allah, alone, without partner, enters paradise)."[16]

8 b) *Man shahida an la ilaha illallah dakhala al-janna* (whoever witnesses that there is no god but Allah alone enters paradise)."[17]

9 *Bashshir al-nasa annahu man qala la ilaha illallahu wahdahu la sharika lahu wajabat lahu al-janna* (announce to the people the tidings that whoever says, 'No god except Allah alone, without partner,' paradise is guaranteed for him)."[18]

10 Uthman ibn Affan said: I heard Allah's Messenger say, "Verily, I know a phrase that no servant utters truthfully from his heart except the fire is made unlawful for him."

---

14 Bukhari narrates this in his *Sahih* (Volume 9, Book 93, Number 601).
15 Narrated by Tirmidhi, *Qiyama* 11; Abu Dawud, *Sunna* 31; Ibn Maja, *Zuhd* 37; and Ahmad 3:213.
16 Narrated by Ibn Adi on the authority of Umar.
17 Al-Bazzar narrates it from Umar.
18 Narrated by al-Nasai from Sahl ibn Hunayf and Zayd ibn Khalid al-Jahni.

Umar ibn al-Khattab said, "I shall tell you what that phrase is. It is the *kalima* of sincerity with which Allah has empowered Muhammad and his Companions, and the *kalima* of fear of Allah that Allah's Prophet (ﷺ) enjoined upon his uncle Abu Talib on his deathbed: the witnessing that there is no god but Allah."[19]

11 Said ibn al-Musayyib relates: When the death of Abu Talib approached, Allah's Apostle came to him and said, "Say, '*La ilaha illallah*,' a word with which I will be able to negotiate or argue (*uhajju*) for you in Allah's presence."[20]

12 a) *Mafatih al-janna shahadatu an la ilaha illallah* (the key to Paradise is witnessing that there is no god but Allah)."[21]

12 b) *Li kulli shayin miftahun wa miftahu al-jannati shahadatu an la ilaha illallah* (everything has its key, and the key to paradise is the witnessing that there is no god but Allah)."[22]

13 Ibn Abbas narrated that the Prophet (ﷺ) said concerning the meaning of the verse *hal jazau al-ihsani illa al-ihsan* (is the reward of goodness anything other than goodness?)" (55:60), "Allah says, 'Can there be any other reward than paradise in the hereafter for one whom I blessed in his worldly life with the recitation of the *kalima* (phrase) of *la ilaha illallah*?" Ikrima and al-Hasan also said that the reward of *la ilaha illallah* can be nothing but paradise.

14 "If anyone comes on the Day of Resurrection who has said *la ilaha illallah* sincerely and with the intention to win Allah's pleasure, Allah will make hellfire forbidden for him."[23]

Tirmidhi comments on the preceding hadith:

19 Ahmad related it in his *Musnad* (1:63 #449).

20 Narrated by Bukhari in his *Sahih* (Volume 8, Book 78, Number 672). Muslim also narrates it in his *Sahih*. Even the "Salafis" have precluded themselves from arguing with the meaning of the above hadith, as they mentioned it in the introduction to their rendering of the Holy Quran. Khan-Hilali translation of the Holy Quran.

21 Ahmad related it from Muadh and Haythami said in *Majma al-zawaid*: "The men in its chain have been declared trustworthy *(thiqa)* although there is interruption in the transmission." It is confirmed by the next hadith.

22 Narrated by Tabarani from Muqal ibn Yasar. Wahb confirmed its authenticity as related in one of the chapter-titles in Bukhari's *Sahih*.

It is narrated from al-Zuhri that he was asked about the Prophet's saying "Whoever says *'La ilaha illallah,'* enters paradise," and he said, "This was only in the beginning of Islam, before the revelation of obligations and the orders and prohibitions."

The *hafiz* Abu Bakr ibn al-Arabi (d. 543) responds saying, "There is no justification for Ibn Shihab's (al-Zuhri) explanation."[24] This is confirmed by the hadith of Utban ibn Malik. Ibn Hajar mentions that al-Zuhri and Said ibn al-Musayyib's opinion was incorrect in light of the hadith of Abu al-Darda and Abu Dharr whereby the Muslim enters paradise "even if he commits adultery or steals." The Prophet (ﷺ) mentioned this specifically to contradict the logic of those who say that great sins will prevent entry into paradise.[25]

15 *Lan yuwafiya abdun yawma al-qiyamati yaqulu la ilaha illallah yabtaghi biha wajh Allah illa harrama Allahu alayhi al-nar* (no servant is true to his word on the Day of Resurrection, saying, 'No god but Allah' in order to seek Allah's good pleasure, except Allah will make the fire unlawful for him)."[26]

16 "The best of my sayings and of the sayings of all prophets before me is, 'There is no god but Allah alone, without partner, to Him belong all sovereignty and glory, and He has power over all things.'"[27]

17 *Afdalu al-amali al-imanu billahi wahdah, thumma al-jihad, thumma hujjatun mabrura, tufdilu sair al-amali kama bayna matla al-shamsi ila maghribiha* (the best deed is belief in Allah alone, then fighting in the way of Allah, then pilgrimage that is accepted. These outweigh all deeds the distance of East to West."[28]

18 *Alaysa yashhadu an la ilaha illallah wa anni rasulullah? Qalu innahu yaqulu dhalika wa ma huwa fi qalbihi. Qala la yashhadu ahadun an la ilaha illallah wa anni rasulullah fa*

---

23 Narrated by Bukhari, vol. 8 p.288 #431.
24 Abu Bakr ibn al-Arabi, *Aridat al-ahwadhi* (10:105).
25 Ibn Hajar, *Fath al-bari, Riqaq* ch. 14 (1989 ed. 11:324).
26 Narrated by Ahmad and Bukhari from Utban ibn Malik.
27 Narrated by Tirmidhi from Amr ibn Shuayb, from his father, from his grandfather (*hasan gharib*).
28 Narrated by Ahmad from Maiz with a sound chain.

yadkhulu al-nara aw tutimuhu. Qala anas fa ajabani hadha al-hadith fa qultu li ibni uktubhu fa katabahu (it is narrated on the authority of Utban ibn Malik that he went to Madina and said, "Something was wrong with my eyesight, so I said to the Prophet (ﷺ), 'It is my ardent desire that you should grace my house with your presence and pray there so that I should take the spot where you prayed as a place of worship).'"

Another version, also in Muslim, has, "I sent for the Prophet (ﷺ) the message, 'Come and lay for me a place for worship' [*khutta li masjidan*]." Imam Nawawi said it means, "Mark for me a spot that I can take as a place for worship by obtaining blessing from your having been there [*mutabarrikan bi atharika*]." Utban ibn Malik continues:

> "So the Prophet (ﷺ) came there, with those of the Companions whom Allah wished. He entered (my home) and performed prescribed prayer. Then the Companions began to talk among themselves about Malik ibn Dukhshum, and they wished that the Prophet (ﷺ) would curse him so that he should die or meet some calamity. After the Prophet (ﷺ/) finished praying he said, 'Does Malik ibn Dukhshum not bear witness to the fact that there is no god but Allah and that I am the Messenger of Allah?' They said, 'Yes, he no doubt says this but it is not in his heart.' The Prophet (ﷺ) replied, 'No-one ever witnesses that there is no god but Allah and that I am Allah's Messenger and then enters the fire or consumes it.'[29]

Anas said, "This hadith impressed me so much that I ordered my son to write it down and he did." Imam Nawawi says, "In this hadith is evidence for obtaining blessings through the relics of saints (*al-tabarruk bi athar al-salihin*)."

19 *Al-imanu bidun wa sabuna baban fa adnaha imatat al-adha an al-tariq wa arfauha qawlu la ilaha illallah* (belief is seventy and some branches. Its lowest branch is the removal of harm from the road while its highest is to say, 'There is no

---

29 Narrated by Muslim.

god but Allah).'"[30]

20 *Man kana akhir kalamihi la ilaha illallah dakhala al-janna* (whoever breathes his last with the words, *la ilaha illallah*, enters paradise)."[31]

Imam Nawawi said:

> The hadith master Abu al-Baqa told us: Hafiz Abu Muhammad informed us: Abu Tahir al-Silafi informed us: Abu Ali al-Burdani said: I heard Hannad ibn Ibrahim al-Nasafi saying: I heard Abu Ishaq Ibrahim ibn Muhammad al-Qattan saying: I heard Abu Abd Allah Umar ibn Ahmad Ibn Ishaq al-Attar saying: I heard Abu Abd Allah Muhammad ibn Muslim ibn Warah al-Razi saying: Abu Hatim Muhammad ibn Idris al-Razi and I were present with Abu Zura al-Razi at the time of his death, so I said to Abu Hatim, "Come, let us remind him to say the *shahada*." Abu Hatim said, "I would be ashamed before Abu Zura to remind him of the *shahada*, but come, let us recall the hadith, perhaps when he hears it he will say it." I started and said: Muhammad ibn Bashshar told us: Abu Asim al-Nabil told us: from Abd al-Hamid ibn Jafar—then I got confused about the hadith as if I never heard it or read it. So Abu Hatim started and said: Muhammad ibn Bashshar told us: Abu Asim al-Nabil told us: from Abd al-Hamid ibn Jafar—then he too got confused as if he never read it or heard it before. Then Abu Zura, may Allah be pleased with him, spoke and said: Muhammad ibn Bashshar told us: Abu Asim al-Nabil told us: Abd al-Hamid ibn Jafar told us: from Salih ibn Abi Urayb: from Kathir ibn Murrah: from Muadh ibn Jabal, may Allah be pleased with him, he said: the Messenger of Allah, may Allah bless him and give him peace, said, "Whoever speaks as his last words: '*La ilaha illallah*'"—then Abu Zura's spirit came out with the letter *ha* (the last letter of the word Allah) before he could say "he will enter paradise." That was in the year 262.[32]

21 *Man mata wa huwa yalamu annahu la ilaha illallah*

---

30 Narrated by Muslim, Tirmidhi, Nasai, Ibn Majah, and Ahmad.

31 Narrated from Muadh by Ahmad, Abu Dawud, and al-Hakim.

32 Nawawi, *al-Tarkhis fi al-ikram bi al-qiyam li dhawi al-fadl wa al-maziyya min ahl al-Islam* (p. 84).

dakhala al-janna (whoever dies knowing full well that there is no god but Allah, enters paradise)."[33]

22 *Idhhab bi nalayya hatayni fa man laqita min waraa hadha al-hait yashhadu an la ilaha illallah mustayqinan biha qalbahu fa bashshirhu bi al-janna* (the Prophet (ﷺ) said to Abu Hurayra, "Go with these two sandals of mine and whoever you meet behind this wall that witnesses that there is no god except Allah with certitude in his heart, give him glad tidings that he will enter paradise)."[34] The latter then met Umar, who prevented him from announcing this to the people, and the Prophet (ﷺ) then agreed with him on the grounds that the people, upon learning of this grace, would rely upon it and forget everything else. The prevention of this news reaching the ears of the ignorant is confirmed by the hadith of Muadh and that of Ubada ibn al-Samit through al-Sunabihi, both narrated by Muslim in the same chapter.[35]

23 *Man shahida an la ilaha illallah wa anna Muhammadan rasulullah harrama Allahu alayhi al-nar* (Abd al-Rahman ibn Usayla al-Sunabihi said: When I entered upon Ubada ibn al-Samit at the time of his death I burst into tears so he said, "Why are you crying? By Allah, if I were asked to testify I would testify for you, and if I were given intercession I would intercede for you, and if it were in my power I would certainly help you! By Allah, I never heard a hadith from Allah's Messenger in which there was benefit for you except I narrated it to you. All but one; and I shall narrate it to you now since I am about to breathe my last. I heard Allah's Messenger say, "Whoever witnesses that there is no god but Allah and that Muhammad is Allah's Messenger, Allah forbids the fire from touching him."[36]

Qadi Iyad said:

> In this hadith is the proof for the permissibility of keeping certain types of knowledge away from the common people due to the inability of their minds to understand it correctly, as long as it does not concern

---

33 Narrated by Muslim and Ahmad from Uthman.
34 Narrated by Muslim from Abu Hurayra.
35 Muslim, Book of *iman* ch. 10.
36 Muslim and Tirmidhi narrated it.

an obligation of religion or stipulations for punishment.[37]

24 *Ya Muadh ibn Jabal ma min ahadin yashhadu an la ilaha illallah wa anni rasulullah sidqan min qalbihi illa harramahu allahu ala al-nar. Qala ya rasulallah afala ukhbiru al-nasa fayastabshiru? Qala idhan yattakilu* (the Prophet (ﷺ) said, "O Muadh ibn Jabal! No one witnesses that there is no god but Allah and that I am Allah's Messenger truthfully from his heart except Allah has made him unlawful for the fire." Muadh said, "O Messenger of Allah, shall I not tell the people so that they will be glad?" He replied, "If you do, they will rely on it (and leave everything else))."[38]

25 *Asadu al-nasi bi shafaati yawma al-qiyama man qala La ilaha illallah khalisan mukhlisan min qalbihi* (Abu Hurayra inquired of the Prophet (ﷺ), "O Messenger of Allah, who will be the most fortunate of people to receive your intercession on the Day of Resurrection?" The Prophet (ﷺ) replied, "O Abu Hurayra, I knew, because of your love of what I say, that no one other than you would ask me of this hadith. The most fortunate of people to receive my intercession on the Day of Resurrection are those who said, *la ilaha illallah* purely and sincerely from the heart)."[39]

26 Usama ibn Zayd killed an idolater in battle after the latter had said, "There is no god but Allah" (*la ilaha illallah*). When news of this reached Allah's Messenger, he condemned Usama in the strongest terms and he said to him, "How can you kill him after he said, '*La ilaha illallah*?'" He replied, "But he said it with the sword hanging over his head." The Prophet (ﷺ) said again, "How can you kill him after he said '*La ilaha illallah*?'" He replied, "O Messenger of Allah, he said it in dissimulation (*taqiyyatan*)." The Prophet (ﷺ) said, "Did you split his heart open (to see)?" He did not cease to reprove him until Usama wished that he had not entered Islam until after he had killed that man so that he might have been forgiven all his past sins through belief.[40]

27 Al-Miqdad said: I asked, "O Messenger of Allah, suppose I

---

37 Nawawi, *Sharh sahih Muslim* (Iman Ch. 10 #47).

38 Narrated by Muslim, Ahmad and Bayhaqi from Anas. Muslim says: "Muadh narrated it at the time of his death to avoid sinning (by keeping it to himself)."

39 Narrated by Bukhari from Abu Hurayra.

40 Narrated by Bukhari, Muslim, Ahmad, Tayalisi, Abu Dawud, Nasai, al-Adni, Abu Awana, al-Tahawi, al-Hakim, and Bayhaqi.

and one of the idolaters battled and he cut off my hand, then I was positioned to strike him and he said, *la ilaha illallah!* Do I kill him or spare him?" He said, "Spare him." I said, "Even if he cut off my hand?" He said, "Even so." I asked him again two or three times whereupon he said, "If you kill him after he says, '*La ilaha illallah*,' then you are like him before he said it, and he is like you before you killed him."[41]

28 *Innallaha la yuadhdhibu min ibadihi illa al-marid wa al-mutamarrid ala Allah wa aba an yaqula la ilaha illallah* (the Prophet (ﷺ) said, "Allah does not punish His servants, except the rebel against Allah who refuses to say, there is no god but Allah)."[42]

29 *Afdalu al-dhikri la ilaha illallah* (the Prophet (ﷺ) said, "The best remembrance of Allah is to say, 'There is no god but Allah).'"[43]

30 *Al-tasbih nusfu al-mizan, wa al-hamdu lillah tamlauhu, wa LA ILAHA ILLALLAH laysa laha duna Allahi hijabun hatta tukhlisu ilayh* (the Prophet (ﷺ) said, "Saying *subhan Allah* (glory to Allah) is half the balance, and saying *al-hamdu lillah* (all praise belongs to Allah) completes the balance, and there is no veil between *la ilaha illallah* and Allah Himself (i.e. it is not even weighed in the Balance); it reaches Him directly."[44]

31 *Kunna inda al-nabiyyi sallallahu alayhi wa sallam fa qala hal fikum gharib? yani ahl al-kitab qulna la ya rasulallah fa amara bi ghalqi al-abwabi wa qala irfau aydikum wa qulu la ilaha illallah! farafana aydina saatan thumma qala al-hamdu lillah! allahumma innaka baathtani bi hadhihi al-kalimai wa waadtani alayha al-jannata wa anta la tukhlifu al-miad! thumma qala abshiru fa innallaha qad ghafara lakum* (Yala ibn Shaddad relates that his father Shaddad ibn Aws told him, as Ubada ibn al-Samit was present and confirmed it, "We were sitting with Allah's Messenger and he asked if there was any stranger—the narrator said, i.e. People of the Book symbol—in the gathering. We said that

41 Narrated by Ahmad, Abu Dawud, Nasai, Shafii in his *Musnad*, and Bayhaqi in the *Shuab*.

42 Ibn Majah narrated it.

43 Tirmidhi (*hasan*), Nasai, Ibn Majah, Ibn Hibban, Bayhaqi in *Shuab al-iman*, from Jabir ibn Abd Allah.

44 Narrated by Tirmidhi from Abd Allah ibn Umar. Suyuti in *al-Jami al-saghir* said it is sound (*sahih*).

there was none. He said, 'Shut the door, raise up your hands and say, "There is no god but Allah."' We raised our hands and recited the *kalima tayyiba* for some time. He then exclaimed, *'al-hamdu lillah!* O Allah, You have sent me with this word and have ordered me to teach it and have promised me paradise for it, and You do not take back Your promise. Be glad, for Allah has forgiven you!'"⁴⁵

32 Abd Allah ibn Salam relates: As we were travelling with Allah's Messenger he heard the people asking, "Which action is the best, O Allah's Messenger?" He said, "Belief in Allah, fighting in Allah's way, and pilgrimage that is accepted." After this he heard a call coming from a valley saying, "I bear witness that there is no god but Allah and that Muhammad is the Messenger of Allah," whereupon he said, "And I bear witness to the same, and I bear witness that no one bears witness to this except he clears himself of *shirk* (associating a partner to Allah)."⁴⁶

33 The Prophet (ﷺ) came out and heard the *adhan*. When he heard the *muadhdhin* say, *la ilaha illallah*, he said, *khalaa al-andad*," which means, "He (the speaker) has denied (the existence of) partners (to Allah)."⁴⁷

34 *Yakhruju min al-nari man qala la ilaha illallah wa kana fi qalbihi min al-khayri ma yazinu shaira, thumma yakhruju min al-nari man qala la ilaha illallah wa kana fi qalbihi min al-khayri ma yazinu badhra, thumman yakhruju min al-nari man qala la ilaha illallah wa kana fi qalbihi min al-khayri ma yazinu dharra* (there will come out of the fire anyone who ever said, 'There is no god but Allah,' and there is in his heart a bead's worth of goodness. Then there will come out of the fire anyone who ever said, 'There is no god but Allah,' and there is in his heart a grain's worth of goodness. Then there will come out of the fire anyone who ever said, 'There is no

---

45 The chain of this hadith is fair *(hasan)*. Narrated from Yala ibn Shaddad's father and Ubada ibn al-Samit by Ahmad, Nasai, Tabarani, al-Hakim, al-Mundhiri in *al-Targhib*, and others. Al-Haythami said in *Majma al-zawaid*: "The sub-narrators in its chain are trustworthy."

46 Ahmad and Tabarani in *al-Awsat* relate it with a sound chain, as stated by Haythami in *Majma al-zawaid*.

47 Ibn Abi al-Dunya narrated it, and Suyuti cites it in his commentary of verse 2:18 in *al-Durr al-manthur*.

god but Allah,' and there is in his heart an atom's worth of goodness."[48]

35 Muadh ibn Jabal said that the last time he spoke with the Prophet (ﷺ), he asked him, "What action is most beloved to Allah?" The Prophet (ﷺ) replied, "That you die with your tongue still moist with the mention (*dhikr*) of Allah."[49]

36 *Ala unabbiukum bi khayri amalikum wa azkaha inda malikikum wa arfaiha fi darajatikum wa khayrin lakum min infaqi al-dhahabi wa al-waraqi wa khayrin lakum min an talqu aduwwakum fa tadribu anaqahum wa yadribu anaqakum qalu bala qala dhikrullah* (the Prophet (ﷺ) said, "Shall I tell you something that is the best of all deeds, constitutes the best act of piety in the eyes of your Lord, will elevate your status in the hereafter, and carries more virtue than the spending of gold and silver or taking part in jihad and slaying and being slain in the path of Allah? It is the *dhikr* or remembrance and mention of Allah)."[50]

37 *Ma amila adamiyyun amalan anja lahu min adhabi al-qabri min dhikrillah* (the Prophet (ﷺ) said, "A human being cannot do anything that is more effective in saving him from the punishment of the grave than the *dhikr* or remembrance of Allah)."[51]

38 Anas reports that the Prophet (ﷺ) was once asked the same question as Muadh in hadith #35, and he replied, "Knowledge of Allah." It was then asked, "And which action adds to this in merit?" He repeated, "Knowledge of Allah." They said, "We ask about actions and you answer concerning knowledge?" The Prophet (ﷺ) said, "A few actions are greatly useful as long as there is knowledge; while a lot of actions

---

48 Related by Bukhari, Muslim, Ahmad, Tirmidhi (*hasan sahih*), Bayhaqi, Nasai, Tabarani, Ibn Majah, and Ibn Khuzayma from Anas.

49 Related by Tabarani and al-Bazzar (*hasan*). Note that hadith #29 stipulates that the best *dhikr* is *la ilaha illallah*.

50 Narrated from Abu al-Darda by Ahmad, Tirmidhi, Ibn Majah, Ibn Abi al-Dunya, al-Hakim (*sahih*), al-Dhahabi (who confirmed al-Hakim), and others.

51 Narrated from Muadh ibn Jabal by Ahmad. Haythami said in *Majma al-zawaid* that the sub-narrators in its chain of transmission are the men of sound hadith, although the *tabii* link is missing; however, Tabarani narrated it through a second chain which is entirely sound (*sahih*). Also narrated with the word *al-abd* (Allah's servant) instead of *adamiyyun* (a human being) by Malik in his *Muwatta*, Tirmidhi, Ibn Majah, al-Hakim (*sahih*), and al-Dhahabi (who confirmed al-Hakim).

are useless if there is ignorance." Anas said, "He spoke of this at length."[52]

This hadith is confirmed by hadith #37, and by the first phrase of hadith #17, whereby "the best deed is belief in Allah alone." The hadith is further confirmed by our decisive knowledge that the purpose of creation is knowledge of Allah. This is indicated by Ibn Abbas' explanation of the verse *wa ma khalaqtu al-jinna wa al-insa illa li yabudun (I did not create the jinn and humankind except to worship* (= know) *Me)"* (51:56), and the verse *falam annahu la ilaha illallah (Know that there is no god except Allah)"* (47:19).

39 *Wal-ladhi nafsi bi yadihi law jia bi al-samawati wa al-ardi wa man fihinna wa ma baynahunna fa wudina fi kaffati al-mizani wa wudiat shahadatu an la ilaha illallahu fi al-kaffati al-ukhra la rajahat bihinna* (by Him in Whose hand is my soul, if the heavens and the earth and all that are in them and everything that is in between were brought and placed in one pan of the Balance, and the witnessing that there is no god but Allah were placed in the other, the latter would outweigh the former)."[53]

40 After the Prophet (ﷺ) passed from this world Abu Bakr said to the Companions, "I asked Allah's Messenger what basic thing was necessary for salvation, and he replied that whoever accepts the Word that I brought, which I offered to my uncle Abu Talib and which he rejected; this Word constitutes salvation for him."[54]

1.5. THE PROPHET'S MERCY TOWARD DISBELIEVERS

Ibn Abbas narrates that the Quraysh said to the Prophet (ﷺ), "Invoke for us your Lord so that He will turn al-Safa mountain into gold for us. Then we will believe." The Prophet

---

52 Ibn Abd al-Barr reports it in *Fadl al-ilm* with a weak chain. See also *Ithaf al-sadat al-muttaqin* (1:85), Suyuti's *al-Durr al-manthur* (2:221), and al-Mundhiri's *al-Tarhib wa al-targhib* (3:525).

53 Related by Tabarani and by Suyuti in *al-Durr al-manthur*. Haythami in *Majma al-zawaid* stated that the sub-narrators in its chain are trustworthy, but that the Tabii link is missing.

54 Related by Ahmad (1:6), Tabarani in *al-Awsat*, Tayalisi in his *Musnad*, Ibn Sad in his *Tabaqat* (2/2:84-85), Abu Yala, Ibn Abi Shayba, Bayhaqi in *Shuab al-iman* (1:107-108 #92-93) and al-Bazzar. See above, hadith #10-11. This hadith is sound although in Ahmad the link between al-Zuhri and Abu Bakr and Uthman is not named

(ﷺ) said, "Will you do truly?" They said yes. Then he began to invoke. Gabriel came to him and said:

> Your Lord sends His greeting to you and says, "If you wish, al-Safa shall become gold for them, and after that, whoever among them disbelieves I shall punish him with a kind of punishment I have never inflicted on anyone in all the worlds; and if you wish, instead I will open for them the gate of repentance and mercy."

> The Prophet (ﷺ) said, "Nay, the gate of repentance and mercy!"[55]

Imam Suyuti cites this hadith as an explanation for the circumstances in which verse 6:109 was revealed; "They swear their strongest oaths by Allah that if a special sign came to them they would believe. Say, 'Certainly all signs are in the power of Allah but what will make you realize that if signs came, they will not believe?'"[56]

Abu Hurayra said the Prophet (ﷺ) was asked, "O Messenger of Allah, invoke Allah's curse on the disbelievers." He replied, "I was not sent as an invoker of curses. I was sent only as a Mercy."[57]

other than "a man from the trustworthy people among the Helpers (ansar)," while Bayhaqi's and Tayalisi's narration from al-Zuhri is from Said ibn al-Musayyib from Abd Allah ibn Amr ibn al-As.

55 Imam Ahmad narrates it in his *Musnad* (1:242) and Ibn al-Jawzi cites it in *al-Wafa* (p. 434, ch. 4 of *Abwab sifatihi al-manawiyya*).

56 Imam Suyuti, *Asbab al-nuzul*

57 Muslim narrates it in his *Sahih*, in the book entitled *Kitab al-birr wa al-sila*.

2. Funeral Prayer in Absentia (SALAT AL-JANAZA ALA AL-GHAIBIN)

2.1. Introduction

Questions addressed in this chapter include:

Is it permissible to perform the funeral prayer for all absent Muslims indiscriminately?

What about Albani's opinion that the funeral prayer in absentia is an innovation?

What is the position of the mainstream scholars on this issue?

2.2. Permissibility of Funeral Prayer in Absentia According to Mainstream Islam

The permissibility of performing the funeral prayer in absentia—i.e. for Muslims who died elsewhere in the world rests on the following hadith.[1] They are cited with excerpts from Nawawi's Commentary on them:

1 Abu Hurayra narrated that the Prophet (ﷺ) announced to the people the death of the Negus (al-Najashi) on the day that he died, then went outside with them to the (open air) place of prayer and said "Allah is Greater!" four times.

Nawawi said:

1 Narrated by Muslim in his *Sahih* (*Kitab al-janaiz*, ch. 22: "On Saying *Allahu akbar* Over the Remains").

Al-Shafii, and those who agree with him, see in this hadith a proof for praying over the absent dead. There is manifest in the hadith a miracle of the Prophet's, due to his proclamation of the Negus' death on the very day that he died in Abyssinia. There is also in the hadith the desirability of proclaiming someone's death, but not in the pre-Islamic fashion that means to glorify and so forth.

Abu Hanifa may have cited the words, "He came outside to the place of prayer" as proof that the funeral prayer is not prayed inside the mosque. However, our school (Shafii) and that of the great majority of the scholars is that it is permissible to perform it inside the mosque . . . The exit is interpreted to signify greater publicity and to show the people the Prophet's great miracle. There is also the (desirable) increase in the number of worshippers. It offers no proof whatsoever that the prayer cannot be prayed inside the mosque. What the scholars have considered prohibited is to bring the remains into the mosque. [2]

2 Abu Hurayra narrated that the Prophet (ﷺ) announced to the people the death of the Negus–the leader of the Abyssinians–on the same day that he died, saying, "Ask forgiveness for your brother." Ibn Shihab (al-Zuhri) said, "Said ibn al-Musayyib also narrated to me that Abu Hurayra narrated to him that the Prophet (ﷺ) arranged them in rows in the place of prayer and prayed saying "Allah is Greater!" four times.

3 Jabir ibn Abd Allah narrated that the Prophet (ﷺ) prayed over As-hama the Negus saying, "Allah is Greater!" four times.

Nawawi said:

Ibn Qutayba said that the meaning of *as-hama* in Arabic is *atiyya*. The scholars have said that al-Najashi–the Negus–is the title of every king of the Abyssinians, while *as-hama* is the name of the righteous king who lived in the time of the Prophet (ﷺ) . . . Ibn Abd al-Barr said, "The consensus has agreed on

---

2 Nawawi, *Sharh sahih Muslim* (al-Mays ed.) 7/8:25-28.

four *takbir*s. That is the agreement of the jurists and those who give legal decisions in all Muslim countries, based on the sound narrations."

4 Jabir ibn Abd Allah said that the Prophet (ﷺ) said, "Today one righteous servant of Allah has died: *as-hama*." Jabir continued, "Then he rose and led us in prayer over him."

5 Jabir ibn Abd Allah said that the Prophet (ﷺ) said, "A brother of yours has died. Therefore rise and pray over him." Jabir continued, "We stood up and he arranged us in two rows."

Nawawi said:

> His words, "Therefore rise and pray over him" indicate the obligatory nature (*wujub*) of the funeral prayer, which is a collective obligation (*fard kifaya*) according to the Consensus.
>
> The correct position in our school (Shafii) is that the obligation of the funeral prayer is fulfilled by the prayer of a single man. It has also been said that the condition of fulfillment is that two men offer it; some said three, some said four.

6 Imran ibn Hisayn narrated that the Prophet (ﷺ) said, "Your brother al-Najashi (the Negus) has died. Therefore pray over him." Imran continued, "Then he stood up and he arranged us in rows behind him, and he prayed over him."[3]

Nawawi said:

> The number of greetings (*salams*) is not mentioned in Muslim's narrations. However, al-Daraqutni mentioned it in his *Sunan* and the consensus of scholars has been to refer to the latter. Their majority said that one gives a single *salam*. Sufyan (al-Thawri), Abu Hanifa, al-Shafii, and a number of the Salaf said that one gives two *salams*.
>
> The scholars differ whether the imam says *salam* aloud or not. Abu Hanifa and al-Shafii say the former, while two opinions are narrated from Malik.

---

3 Muslim narrated it.

The scholars differ as to whether the hands are raised for each *takbir*. The school of al-Shafii stipulates the raising of the hands in each one. This is what Ibn al-Mundhir, who opts for it, reports from Ibn Umar, Umar ibn Abd al-Aziz, Ata, Salim ibn Abd Allah, Qays ibn Abi Hazim, al-Zuhri, al-Awzai, Ahmad, and Ishaq (ibn Rahawayh or Rahuwyah). Ibn al-Mundhir reports from al-Thawri, Abu Hanifa, and the latter's school, that the hands are raised only in the first *takbir*. From Malik are reported three opinions: the hands are raised in all four; the hands are raised in the first only; the hands are not raised in any of the four.

2.3. ALBANI LABELS FUNERAL PRAYER IN ABSENTIA INNOVATION

Albani says:

> It [funeral prayer over every Muslim in absentia] is among the innovations in religion of which no one doubts, among those who know the *sunna* of the Prophet (ﷺ) and the school (*madhhab*) of the Salaf.[4]

It would be enough for one to know that the true Salaf had more than a single school of law (*madhhab*) to help them realize the strangeness of Albani's opinion. It is known that al-Shafii and Ahmad, who were of the Salaf, and their schools permitted the in absentia funeral prayer for one and all, indiscriminately. The above *fatwa* is all the more peculiar in light of the fact that it concludes a section of the book that begins with the author's own declaration that:

> The funeral (*janaza*) prayer is lawful over . . . those who died in a country where they have no one to pray over them in their presence. Muslims pray over such people in absentia (*salat al-ghaib*), because of the Prophet's prayer over the Negus (al-Najashi).[5]

---

4 M. Nasir al-Din al-Albani, *Talkhis ahkam al-janaiz* (s.n.: Jamiyyat ihya al-turath al-islami, n.d. [reprint of the 1st edition, Amman: al-Maktabat al-Islamiyah, 1982]) p. 48.

5 *Ibid.* p. 44, 47.

2.4. MAINSTREAM ISLAMIC VIEW ON ALBANI'S *FATWA*

He then reduces this general permission to a selective one whereby the in absentia prayer may be offered for some, but not all. What is his proof for this?

First he quotes Ibn al-Qayyim's words, "It was not part of the Prophet (ﷺ)'s guidance or his *sunna* to pray on every single dead in absentia, for a great deal of the Muslims died in absentia and he did not pray over them, and it is true that he prayed the funeral prayer over the Negus."[6]

Second, then he asserts, "When the rightly-guided caliphs and other caliphs died, none of the Muslims prayed the funeral prayer in absentia over them, and if they had, the reports about it would have been transmitted from them from every side."

Neither statement constitutes proof that the in absentia *janaza* for all Muslims "is among the innovations in religion of which no one doubt among those who know the *sunna* of the Prophet (ﷺ) and the school (*madhhab*) of the Salaf." Ibn al-Qayyim's own school contradicts him, since Ibn Qudama explicitly precluded any condition to the funeral prayer in absentia; he says it is permissible regardless of number, social status, or whether the absent ones died in a Muslim environment or not.[7]

The same universality is emphasized by Ibn al-Jawzi before him in his book of comparative *fiqh*, in the section entitled, "The funeral prayer in absentia may be performed with the proper intention, contrary to (the opinions of) Abu Hanifa and Malik."[8] *Fiqh al-sunna* does not say otherwise.[9] The fact that the rightly-guided caliphs, or the Caliphs who succeeded them, omitted something does not constitute proof that *janaza* in absentia is against the *sunna*. This is especially true since plain evidence to the contrary is given by the Prophet (ﷺ) himself—provided that the *sunna* instituted by him has not been abrogated, which it has not. At most, the two purported proofs suggest that it is not obligatory to pray the funeral prayer in absentia for every Muslim.

---

6 Ibn al-Qayyim al-Jawziyya, *Zad al-maad* (ed.? 1:205-206).
7 Ibn Qudama, *Mughni ala mukhtasar al-Khiraqi* (Beirut, 1414/1994 ed.) 2:323.
8 Ibn al-Jawzi, *al-Tahqiq fi ahadith al-khilaf* (Beirut, 1414/1994 ed.) 2:14.
9 Sayyid Sabiq, *Fiqh al-sunna* (Cairo, 1408/1987 ed.) 1:352.

2.5. IBN QUDAMA'S PERMISSIBILITY OF FUNERAL PRAYER IN ABSENTIA

Ibn Qudama said:[10]

[The position of the Hanbali school:] The funeral prayer over the dead who are in another locality is permissible with the proper intention. One faces the *qibla* and prays as in the presence of the body, regardless whether the absent dead is in the direction of the *qibla* or not, or whether the distance between the respective countries warrants shortening the prayer during travel or not. This is also Shafii's position. According to Malik and Abu Hanifa, it is not permissible. [Ibn Abi Musa did relate from Ahmad another opinion that resembles theirs.] For, according to them, one of the prerequisites of the funeral prayer is the presence of the body, since the prayer is not allowed to take place within the locality where the body is not present.

Supporting our position is that it was narrated that the Prophet (ﷺ) proclaimed the death of the Negus, the leader of the Abyssinians, the day that he died, led the Companions in prayer in the place of prayer outdoors, and uttered four *takbir*s. The hadith is agreed upon. If it is objected that it is possible that the earth was contracted so that the Prophet (ﷺ) could see the Negus' remains, we reply that this was not reported, and if it had been the case he would have certainly told us.

Also supporting our position is that we follow the Prophet (ﷺ) [indiscriminately] as long as it is not established that he alone is allowed to carry out this practice (i.e. that it concerns a practice allowed exclusively for him). Since it is not permissible to pray over the *janaza* from a far distance, even if one can see him, and if the Prophet (ﷺ) had seen the Negus, the funeral prayer (in absentia) would have been particular to the Prophet (ﷺ) himself. However, he lined up the Companions and led them in prayer.

If it is objected, "There was no one among the Abyssinians to pray over him," we reply, your school (Hanafi and Maliki) does not provide for the funeral

---

10 Ibn Qudama, *al-Mughni, Kitab al-janaiz*, section entitled "Whoever misses the prayer offers it at the grave" (Beirut, 1414/1994 ed.).

prayer in such a case, for you do not allow the prayer over the victim of drowning, the prisoner of war (who dies while in captivity by non-Muslims), and the one who dies in the wilderness, even if there is no one to pray over them. Furthermore, this is far-fetched, because the Negus was the king of the Abyssinians and had entered Islam and shown his Islam. Therefore it is unlikely that there was no one to pray over him.

Section #1: If the dead person is in one of the two extremities of the city, it is not allowed for someone who resides on the other side to pray over him in absentia. He has to go to the side of the city where the body is. The author [Umar ibn al-Husayn al-Khiraqi, d. 334] said that this was the preference of Abu Hafs al-Barmaki. The reason is that it is possible, in such a case, to be in the presence of the *janaza* and perform the prayer over him or at the grave. However, Abu Abd Allah ibn Hamid prayed over a man who died on one side of Baghdad while he himself was on the other side. The dead man was far away, and the prayer in absentia therefore became permissible for him, as if he prayed over someone in a different city. The permissibility in this case is related to the city where he resides.

Section #2: The allowed time span for the funeral prayer in absentia is one month, like the funeral prayer over the grave. This is because it is not certain that the remains do not decompose after that time. Ibn Aqil said, concerning the one eaten by a wild beast and the victim of fire, that it is possible not to pray over them due to their disappearance in a different fashion than the one who is missing or the victim of drowning, for something remains over which to pray in the case of the latter. Finally, the prayer can be done over someone who belongs in one of these categories—short of ritual washing—as long as he is recognized, just as is done for the absent one who is in a far place. In such cases they are exempt from washing due to impediments. This is similar to the case of someone who is living, but unable to wash or perform dry ablution (*tayammum*); he must perform prayer according to his condition.[11]

11 *Ibid.* 2:323.

3. DONATING ONE'S REWARD TO A DECEASED (*IHDA AL-THAWAB ILA AL-MAYT*)

3.1. INTRODUCTION

Questions addressed in this chapter include:

What is the understanding of the reliable mainstream scholars of the Community on donating one's reward to a deceased (*ihda al-thawab ila al-mayt*), especially the following issues:

Can one donate the reward of Quranic recitation to the dead?

Can one address the dead upon burial with the *kalima tayyiba*, *LA ILAHA ILLALLAH MUHAMMADUN RASULULLAH*?

Can one recite from the Quran on a grave, since the Prophet (ﷺ) said to recite *Surah Ya Sin* on the dead?

What evidence is there from the Quran and hadith on the above points?

What about Imam Tahawi's statement that "There is benefit for dead people in the supplication and alms-giving of the living," and Ibn al-Qayyim's position on these issues?

3.2. DONATING THE REWARD FOR QURANIC RECITATION TO A DECEASED (*IHDA THAWAB AL-QURAN ILA AL-MAYT*)

Donation of all kinds of acts of worship, among them

Quranic recitation, can and do benefit the dead, just as a Muslim's simple supplication does. The true Salaf believed the dead were helped and relieved by the living, as shown by Abu Hurayra's supplication for the dead: *allahumma in kana muhsinan fa zid fi ihsanihi wa in kana musian fa tajawaz an sayyiatihi*—"O Allah, if he did good, then increase his goodness, and if he did evil, then forgive his evil deeds."[1] Moreover, it is established that the best supplication is the opening chapter of the Quran, *Surah Fatiha*, itself.

3.3. THE "SALAFIS" INCORRECT REJECTION OF RECITATION FOR A DECEASED

Nasir al-Din Albani, lists among the rejected innovations in religion,[2] "The recitation of the Quran for the dead and over them,"[3] "recitation of *Surah Fatiha*, for the dead," of "recitation of *Surah Ya Sin* over the graves,"[4] and "donation to deceased Muslims of the reward of acts of worship such as the recitation of the Quran."[5] The "Salafi" condemnation of donating the reward of Quranic recitation to the deceased is further evidence of their exaggerated and sectarian approach, and their deviation from the method and teachings of mainstream Islam. Their condemnation is reminiscent of the Mutazila position, whereby nothing we do can benefit the dead.

3.4. RECITATION FOR A DECEASED ENCOURAGED BY MAINSTREAM ISLAM

The following pages present the authentic mainstream Islamic teaching of the major schools, whereby recitation of the Quran for and over the dead, especially the recitation of *Surah Ya Sin*, is ordered by the Prophet (ﷺ). Mainstream Islamic teaching also holds that donating the reward of acts of worship, such as the recitation of the Quran, to deceased Muslims is not only permitted, but recommended.

There are thus three parts to this exposition:

---

1 Malik narrated it.

2 Shaykh Nasir al-Din Albani, in his book on the rulings that pertain to funerals *(Talkhis ahkam al-janaiz)* published by Jamiyyat ihya al-turath al-islami.

3 *Ibid*. p. 104 #123, #126.

4 *Ibid*. p. 105 #147, #148.

5 *Ibid*. p. 106 #160.

- Reciting from the Quran at a grave (*qiraa ala al-qabr*)
- Donating the reward of Quranic recitation to the dead (*ihda al-thawab*)
- Instructing the dead after burial (*talqin al-mayyit*)

3.4.1. RECITING FROM THE QURAN AT A GRAVE (*QIRAA ALA AL-QABR*)

The Prophet (ﷺ) said, "*Iqrau ala mawtakum ya sin* (recite [*Sura*] *ya sin* over those of you who are dying/deceased)." It is narrated by Abu Dawud,[6] al-Nasai,[7] Ibn Majah,[8] and Ibn Hibban, and he declared it sound (*sahih*).[9]

Abd al-Haqq ibn al-Kharrat al-Ishbili (d. 582) said, "The meaning of this hadith may be that the recitation is done over the person at the time the person is dying; or that it is done at his grave."[10] Al-Qurtubi said the same, according to Suyuti who adds, "I say, the vast majority of the scholars take the former meaning, while Ibn Abd al-Wahid al-Maqdisi al-Hanbali [and others] takes the latter in the monograph he compiled on the topic. Both apply."[11] Ibn Qayyim al-Jawziyya also prefers the former meaning ("dying").[12]

The Prophet (ﷺ) said, "*Ya sin* is the heart of the Quran. No person recites [or reads] it desiring Allah and the afterlife except he is forgiven. Recite [read] it over your dying/deceased."[13]

Ata ibn Abi Rabah said:

> I heard Ibn Umar say: I heard the Prophet (ﷺ) say, "When one of you dies do not tarry, but make haste and take him to his grave, and let someone read at his head the opening of *Surah al-Baqara*, and at his feet its closure when he lies in the grave."[14]

6 Abu Dawud, *Sunan (Janaiz)*.
7 Al-Nasai, *Sunan (Amal al-yawm wal-layla)*.
8 Ibn Majah, *Sunan (Janaiz)*.
9 Ibn Hibban, *Sahih (Ihsan)*.
10 Abd al-Haqq ibn al-Kharrat al-Ishbili, *al-Aqiba* (p. 255 #576).
11 Suyuti, *Sharh al-sudur* p. 312.
12 Ibn Qayyim al-Jawziyya, *Kitab al-ruh* (Madani ed. p. 18-19).
13 Ahmad relates it in his *Musnad* (5:26) as part of a longer narration whose chain contains two unnamed narrators.
14 Al-Tabarani narrates it in *al-Mujam al-kabir*, but Haythami said in *Majma al-zawaid* (3:44) that the latter's chain contains Yahya ibn Abd Allah al-Dahhak al-Babalti who is weak. However, the hadith is confirmed by the practice of Abd Allah ibn Umar as narrated through sound chains (see below). Al-Khallal also narrates this hadith in his *al-Amr bi al-maruf* (p. 122 #239).

It is related that al-Ala ibn al-Lajlaj said to his children:

> When you bury me, say as you place me in the side-opening (*lahd*) of the grave, '*Bismillah wa ala millati rasul Allah* (in the name of Allah and according to the way of Allah's Messenger)." Then flatten the earth over me, and recite [read] at the head of my grave the beginning of *Surah al-Baqara* and its end, for I have seen that Ibn Umar liked it.[15]

Abu Bakr al-Khallal (d. 311) relates the above with the wording, "Flatten the earth over me, then recite [read] at the head of my grave the Opening of the Book, the beginning of *Surah al-Baqara*, and its end, for I have heard Ibn Umar instruct it."[16]

Ali ibn Musa al-Haddad said:

> I was once with Ahmad ibn Hanbal at a funeral in the company of Muhammad ibn Qudama al-Jawhari. After the dead was interred a blind man came up and recited [from the Quran] beside the grave. 'O So-and-so,' Ahmad said to him, 'Recitation at the graveside is an innovation (*bida*)!' But when we left the cemetery Muhammad ibn Qudama asked Ahmad, 'O Abu Abd Allah, what is your opinion of Mubashshir ibn Ismail al-Halabi?' 'A sound authority,' he said, 'have you written anything down from him?' . . . 'Yes,' he replied, 'Mubashshir ibn Ismail related to me on the authority of his father, on the authority of Abd al-Rahman ibn al-Ala' ibn al-Lajlaj, on the authority of his father, that he had requested that upon his death the opening and closing verses of the Chapter of the Cow should be recited over his grave, saying, I heard Ibn

---

15 Narrated by Bayhaqi in *al-Sunan al-kubra* (4:56), Ibn Qudama in *al-Mughni* (2:474, 2:567, 1994 ed. 2:355), al-Tabarani in *al-Kabir*, and Haythami said in *Majma al-zawaid* (3:44) that the latter's narrators were all declared trustworthy.

16 Abu Bakr al-Khallal, *al-Amr bi al-maruf* (p. 121 #237). Ibn Qayyim al-Jawziyya cites it in *Kitab al-ruh* (Madani ed. p. 17) from Khallal's narration in *al-Jami* but without mention of the *Fatiha*.

17 Narrated by al-Ghazali in his *Ihya*, book of "The Remembrance of Death and the Afterlife," trans. T. J. Winter (Cambridge: Islamic Texts Society, 1989) p. 117. Al-Khallal narrates it in *al-Amr bi al-maruf* (p. 122 #240-241), Ibn Qudama in *al-Mughni* (2:567, Beirut 1994 ed. 2:355) and Qalaji in *Fiqh Ibn Umar* (p. 618). Ibn Qayyim al-Jawziyya cites it in *Kitab al-ruh* (Madani ed. p. 18; English translation, KAZI Publications distribution of the Great Books of the Islamic World series) from Khallal's narration in *al-Jami*. Ghazali prefaces the relation with the words: **"There is no harm in reciting the the Quran at graves."**

Umar requesting that this be done.' Thereupon, Ahmad said to him, 'Return to the man, and bid him recite.'"[17]

Nawawi said, "We also narrated in Bayhaqi's *Sunan* (4:56-57) with a fair (*hasan*) chain that Ibn Umar liked for the beginning and the end of *Surah al-Baqara* to be recited over the grave after burial."[18]

Al-Jazari instructed, "Let one recite over the grave, after burial, the beginning of *Surah al-Baqara* and its end."[19] This is based on Ibn Umar's words, narrated by Bayhaqi, "I like that the beginning of *Surah al-Baqara* and its end be recited [read] at the grave."[20] Shawkani comments:

> Nawawi declared its chain fair (*hassana isnadahu*), and even if it is only Ibn Umar's saying, such as this is not uttered on the basis of mere opinion. It is possible that because of what he learned of the benefit of such recitation generally speaking, he then deemed it desirable that it be recited [read] over the grave due to its merit, in the hope that the deceased benefit from its recitation.

Mujalid said al-Shubi said, "The Helpers (*ansar*), if someone died among them, would go to his grave and recite the Quran there."[21]

Yaqub ibn al-Sayyid Ali al-Hanafi said:

> [One visiting the graves] should recite *Surah Ya Sin* or whatever is easy for him to recite from the Quran. Know that Abu Hanifa, may Allah have mercy upon him, considered it blameworthy (*makruh*) to recite the Quran at the cemetery, but not Muhammad (☙).[22]

Qadi Khan al-Hanafi said in his *Fatawa*:

---

18 Nawawi, *Kitab al-adhkar* (Taif ed. p. 212 #493).
19 Cited by Shawkani in *Tuhfat al-dhakirin* (p. 229), from *al-Hisn al-hasin* .
20 Bayhaqi, *Sunan* (4:56).
21 Al-Khallal narrates it in *al-Amr bi al-maruf* (p. 123 #244) with a chain that contains Sufyan ibn Waki who is weak according to Haythami, but from whom Tirmidhi, Ibn Majah, and Ahmad took over eighty narrations. Furthermore Ibn Qayyim al-Jawziyya also cites it as evidence in *Kitab al-ruh* (Madani ed. p. 18).
22 Yaqub ibn al-Sayyid Ali al-Hanafi, *Mafatih al-jinan sharh shirat al-Islam* p. 580.

> If the intention of whoever recites from the Quran
> over the graves be the familiarity of the sound of the
> Quran reaching a deceased, then let him recite. If he
> did not intend that, then Allah hears the Quran wher-
> ever you recite it.[23]

Al-Zafarani said, "I asked al-Shafii about reciting the Quran at the graveside and he said, "*La basa bihi* (there is no harm in it).'"[24]

Ibrahim ibn Rahawayh said, "There is no harm in reciting the Quran in cemeteries."[25]

Imam Ahmad said the same.[26]

Al-Khallal said, Abu Ali al-Hasan ibn al-Haytham al-Bazzar, our most trustworthy shaykh, narrated to me, "I saw Ahmad ibn Hanbal pray behind a blind man who was reciting Quran over the graves."[27]

Nawawi said, "Whoever visits a grave, let him greet its dweller, recite some Quran, and make an invocation for the deceased."[28]

He also said, "It is desirable (*yustahabb*) that one who is visiting the graves recite from the Quran what is easy for him to recite, after which, that he invoke Allah on their behalf. Shafii stipulated it and his companions all agreed with him." In another place he says, "If they conclude the recitation of the Quran over the grave it is better."[29]

Nawawi also said in his *Sharh Sahih Muslim*, "The scholars have declared desirable (*mustahabb*) the recitation of the Quran over the grave."[30]

Al-Qurtubi said, "As for reciting over the grave, then our

23 Suyuti mentions it in *Sharh al-sudur* (p. 312).

24 Al-Khallal narrates it in *al-Amr bi al-maruf* (p. 123 #243), Suyuti in *Sharh al-sudur* (p. 311), and Ibn Qayyim al-Jawziyya in *Kitab al-ruh* (Madina ed. p. 18).

25 Al-Khallal narrates it with his chain (p. 123 #245).

26 Ibn Qudama relates it in *al-Mughni* (1994 ed. 2:355).

27 Ibn Qudama relates it in *al-Mughni* (1994 ed. 2:355) as well as al-Khallal himself with his chain in his book *al-Amr bi al-maruf* (p. 123 #242).

28 Al-Nawawi, *Minhaj al-Talibin*, end of *Kitab al-janaiz*.

29 Nawawi, *al-Majmu sharh al-muhadhdhab*. Suyuti mentioned both excerpts in his *Sharh al-sudur* (p. 311).

30 Nawawi, *Sharh sahih Muslim*, al-Mays ed. 3/4:206.

31 Suyuti mentioned it in his *Sharh al-sudur* (p. 311).

companions (Malikis) are categorical that it is lawful, and others say the same."[31]

Al-Jaziri said, "Someone who visits the grave must engage in *dua* and supplication. He must reflect upon those who died and he must recite Quran for the dead, for the more correct view is that this benefits the dead."[32]

One of the false rulings given by Albani concerning recitation at the graveside is that it is an innovation to recite upon throwing the first earth into the grave (*minha khalaqnakum*), upon throwing the second (*wa fiha nuidukum*), and upon throwing the third (*wa minha nukhrijukum taratan ukhra*). *"From it (the earth) We created you and into it We return you and from it We shall bring you out once more"* (20:55).[33] The proof that this is a hasty and careless ruling is:

1 Even if the chain of the hadith stating that the Prophet (ﷺ) did it, which al-Hakim narrated as well as his student Bayhaqi, was declared weak by Ibn Hajar, it does not eliminate the possibility that the hadith is authentic, and this possibility precludes its practice from being an innovation or being called one.[34]

2 Albani's ruling that it is an innovation contradicts the mainstream Islamic scholars who never came to his conclusion, although they looked at the same evidence—not al-Hakim, Bayhaqi, Ibn Hajar, Ibn al-Jazari, Shawkani, or Nawawi.

Not only did Nawawi not declare this practice an innovation, but he declared it *mustahabb*, or desirable, according to the vast majority of the authorities in the Shafii school.[35]

Nawawi said in *Kitab al-adhkar*:

The *sunna* for whoever is at the graveside [at the time of burial] is to throw earth with his hand three times into the grave at the side of the head.

A large group of our companions [in the Shafii

32 Al-Jaziri, *al-Fiqh ala al-madhahib al-arbaa* (2:540).
33 Albani, *Talkhis ahkam al-janaiz* (p. 102 #90).
34 Al-Hakim, *Mustadrak*.
35 As Shawkani reported in his *Tuhfat al-dhakirin* (p. 229) and *Nayl al-awtar* (4:81) without contradicting him, although he did report Ibn Hajar's grading in the latter.

school] said, "It is desirable (*mustahabb*) that one recite upon throwing the first earth into the grave (*minha khalaqnakum*), upon throwing the second (*wa fiha nuidukum*), and upon throwing the third (*wa minha nukhrijukum taratan ukhra*). *"From it (the earth) We created you / and into it We return you / and from it We shall bring you out once more"* (20:55).

It is desirable that after burial they sit at graveside for the time it takes to slaughter a camel and distribute its meat, and that during that time the sitters busy themselves with reciting the Quran, supplicating for the deceased, exhorting, and telling the stories of the People of Goodness as well as the states of the saints . . . We narrated in *Sahih Muslim* [book of iman] from Amr ibn al-As that he said, "After you bury me, stay around my grave for the duration of slaughtering a camel and distributing its meat, so that I may share your familiar company and examine what I should reply to my Lord's envoys [the angels of the grave]."

We also narrated in *Sunan Abi Dawud* [*Janaiz* #3221] and al-Bayhaqi [*al-Sunan al-kubra* 4:56; also al-Hakim's *Mustadrak* 1:370]: from Uthman that the Prophet (ﷺ), whenever he finished burying the deceased, would stand over him and say: "Ask forgiveness for your brother, and ask for him to be made firm, for he is presently being questioned."

Al-Shafii and his companions said, "It is desirable (*yustahabb*) that they recite something of the Quran at the graveside," and they said, "If they recited the entire Quran it would be good."

We also narrated in Bayhaqi's *Sunan* (4:56-57) with a fair (*hasan*) chain that Ibn Umar liked for the beginning and the end of *Surah al-Baqara* to be recited over the grave after burial.[36]

It is worth noting that the *Aqida al-tahawiyya* states:

Point 89: There is benefit for dead people in the supplication and alms-giving of the living.

This supplication for the dead is an established part of belief transmitted to us by the Khalaf from the Salaf. Now, because Albani has rejected this as an

36 Bayhaqi, *Sunan,* Taif ed. p. 211-212.

innovation, it seems that the "Salafis" are willing to "improve" the *aqida* of Imam al-Tahawi (and the Salaf) by modifying the text to reflect their belief. This is evident in Suhaib Hassan's translation of *Aqida al-Tahawiyya* entitled The Muslim Creed, in which he translates:

> Point 89: The dead benefit from the deeds of their lives, such as prayer and acts of charity[!][37]

Suhaib Hasan has completely mistranslated this point, and implies the opposite of what is actually meant so that it conforms with "Salafi" beliefs. A person might like to give him the benefit of the doubt and say that he made a mistake, but one wonders how such a grave mistake could be made in such a short, fundamental text. Worse yet, how was it then allowed to go to print, as Suhaib Hasan is not only an experienced and meticulous translator, but further specializes in the even more technical translation of hadith? Therefore, this is a clear case of deliberate tampering.

Tahawi's original text says:

> *Wa fi dua al-ahya li al-amwat wa sadaqatihim manfaatun li al-amwat*[38] (in the supplication of the living and their acts of charity there is benefit for the dead).

It is clear that in his translation, Suhaib Hasan changed the words "the supplication of the living" to "the deeds of their lives."

It has already been discussed how the "Salafis" tampered with the text of Nawawi's *Adhkar*. This is only one of many additional examples of the corruption of classical mainstream Islamic texts by the "Salafis."

3.4.2. DONATING THE REWARD OF QURANIC RECITATION TO THE DEAD
(*IHDA THAWAB AL-QURAN ILA AL-MAYT*)

Al-Kamal ibn al-Humam al-Hanafi stated that every single act of worship, including Quran-recitation, can be offered to the deceased.[39] The Hanafi *faqih* Uthman ibn Ali ibn Mihjan al-

---

37 Taken from Iqbal Ahmed Azami's translation of *Aqida al-tahawiyya*.
38 Suhaib Hasan, *The Muslim Creed*, 1991 ISSN 0952-7834.
39 Al-Kamal ibn al-Humam al-Hanafi, *Fath al-qadir*.

Zaylai said:

> There is nothing rationally far-fetched in some-
> one else's reward reaching the dead, because it is
> nothing more than one man's placing what reward he
> possesses at someone else's disposal. Allah is the One
> Who conveys it, and He is able to do that. Nor is this
> specific to one act of worship to the exclusion of oth-
> ers.

Ibn Abidin said that in visiting the graves one may recite:[40]

> *Surah al-Fatiha*
> *Surah al-Baqara*, beginning, *ayat al-kursi*, and
>   *amana al-rasul*
> *Surah Ya Sin*
> *Surah al-Mulk*
> *Surah al-Takathur*
> *Surah al-Ikhlas* 12 or 11 or 7 or 3 times
> Then let him say, "*Allahumma awsil thawaba ma
> qaratuhu ila fulan aw ilayhim* (O Allah, convey the
> reward of what I have recited to so-and-so [one or
> many])."[41]

Makhluf reports that, among the later Malikis, the preferred position is that the reward of Quranic recitation does
reach the deceased. Ibn Rushd states that there is no objection
on the permissibility of donating the reward.[42]
    Imam Suyuti states:

> There is disagreement as to the reward of recita-
> tion reaching to the dead. The vast majority of the
> Salaf, as well as the Three Imams, consider that it
> does reach them, while our Imam, al-Shafii, differs.
> His basis was the verse, *"Wa an laysa li al-insani illa
> ma saa* (the human being can have nothing but what
> he strives for)" (53:39). However, the Salaf replied to
> this objection in several ways:
>   1 The verse is abrogated by Allah's saying, 'Wa al-

---

40 Ibn Abidin, *Hashiyat al-durr al-mukhtar.*
41 Hasanayn Muhammad Makhluf mentioned all these sayings in his *Fatawa shariyya* (2:277-279, 2:308).
42 *Ibid.* 2:300, as stated by Ibn Farhun according to Ibn Abi Zayd al-Qayrawani in his *Risala.*

ladhina amanu wa ittabaathum dhurriyyatuhum (*and those who believe and whose families follow them in faith–to them We shall join their families. Nor shall We deprive them of the fruit of anything of their works. Yet each individual is in pledge for his deeds*" (52:21). This verse enters the children into paradise because of the righteousness of the parents.

2 The verse "The human being can have nothing but what he strives for" is specific to Abraham's and Moses' nations. As for this Community which has been granted mercy, then it has both what it strove for and what was striven for on its behalf. This is the saying of Ikrima.[43]

3 What is meant by "human being" in that verse is the disbeliever. As for the believer, he has both what he strove for and what was striven for on his behalf. This is the saying of (the *tabii*) al-Rabi ibn Anas (d. 139).

4 The human being can have nothing but what he strives for, according to divine justice (*adl*). As for what comes through divine munificence (*fadl*), it is permissible for him that Allah increase him in anything whatsoever. This is the saying of al-Husayn ibn al-Fadl.[44]

5 The meaning of the verse is, "The human being will have nothing counted against him except what he strove for."

They used as proof, of the reward of recitation reaching the dead, the analogy of all that is sent in way of: supplication (*dua*), charity (*sadaqa*), fasting (*sawm*), pilgrimage (*hajj*), and manumission (*itq*), since there is no difference in the transfer of reward whether it is for pilgrimage, charity, endowment (*waqf*), supplication, or recitation. They have also used the hadith that will be mentioned, even if these are weak, yet their collective relevance is that the donation of reward has a basis in the law. Another proof they have used is the fact that the Muslims never ceased at any time in history to gather and recite (the Quran) for their dead without anyone

43 Ibn Abbas' freedman and the transmitter of his *Tafsir*. Bukhari included 139 of his narrations in his *Sahih*. He died in Madina in 104.

44 Al-Bajali, one of Bayhaqi's (d. 458) shaykhs. Qurtubi often cites him in his *Tafsir*.

objecting, and this constitutes consensus (*ijma*). All the above was mentioned by the hadith master (*hafiz*) Shams al-Din ibn Abd al-Wahid al-Maqdisi al-Hanbali in a monograph he compiled on the topic.[45]

Muhammad ibn Ahmad al-Marwazi said:

I once heard Ahmad ibn Hanbal say, "Whenever you enter a cemetery, recite the Opening Chapter of the Book, the Two Refuge-taking Chapters, and [the chapter which begins] '*Say, He is God, the One.*' Make the reward of all this over to the people of the cemetery, for it will reach them."[46]

Ibn Abbas narrates:

The Prophet (ﷺ) once passed by two graves and said, "These two persons are being tortured not for any major sin. One of them never saved himself from being soiled with his urine, while the other used to spread calumnies." The Prophet (ﷺ) then took a green date-palm stalk, split it into two pieces, and fixed one on each grave. They said, "O Allah's Apostle! Why have you done so?" He replied, "I hope that their punishment might be lessened until these two pieces become dry."[47]

Nawawi said, in commenting on the above:

The scholars have declared desirable—*mustahabb* – the recitation of the Quran over the grave due to the above hadith, because if relief from punishment is hoped for through the glorification of date-palm stalks, then the recitation of the Quran is more deserving yet, and Allah knows best.[48]

Qurtubi said:

45 Shams al-Din ibn Abd al-Wahid al-Maqsidi al-Hanbali, *Sharh al-sudur bi sharh hal al-mawta wa al-qubur* (p. 310).

46 Narrated by Abd al-Haqq ibn al-Kharrat al-Ishbili (d. 582) in his book *al-Aqiba*, also by al-Muhibb al-Tabari and Suyuti in *Sharh al-sudur* (p. 312). See also Ghazali's *Ihya*, book of "The Remembrance of Death and the Afterlife," trans. T.J. Winter (Cambridge: Islamic Texts Society, 1989) p. 117.

47 Bukhari and Muslim narrated it. (Cf. (English Bukhari, Volume 1, Book 4, Number 217).

48 Nawawi, *Sharh sahih Muslim* (al-Mays ed. 3/4:206).

It is also said that the reward of recitation goes to the reciter while the reward of listening goes to the deceased, whence mercy reaches him. Allah said, "*If the Quran is recited, listen to it and be silent, perhaps you will be granted mercy*" (7:204). It is not unlikely that in Allah's munificence the reward of both the recitation and the audition reach him, and, added to that, the reward of whatever is donated to him from the recitation even what is not heard, such as charity and supplication . . . Some of our scholars have inferred a proof for the deceased's benefit in the recitation of Quran at the grave from the hadith of the date-palm stalk which the Prophet (ﷺ) split and fixed (above the graves) saying, "Perhaps their punishment might be lessened until these two pieces become dry."

Al-Khattabi said:

Among the People of Knowledge this is understood on the basis that all things make glorification as long as they are in their original state, or their verdancy and freshness; until they lose their moistness or greenness, or they are cut off from their root.

Someone other than Khattabi said, "If the glorification of the stalk lightens their punishment, what about the recitation of the Quran by the believer? This hadith also constitutes a legal basis for the planting of trees at the site of graves." Among the Companions, it is established that Abu Barza al-Aslami[49] and Burayda[50] asked to be buried together with two fresh stalks.[51]

Ibn al-Jawzi said, as reported by Ahmad ibn Qudama al-Maqdisi, "Let whoever visits the graves face towards the deceased in his grave, recite something from the Quran, and donate it to him, and let the visit be on Friday (the day of *juma*)."[52]

Nawawi said:

There is consensus among the scholars that *dua*

---

49 As narrated by Ibn Asakir through Hammad ibn Salama.
50 As narrated by Ibn Sad.
51 Suyuti mentioned this in *Sharh al-sudur* (p. 312-313).
52 Ahmad ibn Qudama al-Maqsidi, in his abridgment entitled *Mukhtasar minhaj al-qasidin* (p. 448).

[invocation] for the dead benefits them, and that its reward reaches them. They have adduced Allah's saying. "*And those who came (into the faith) after them say, Our Lord! Forgive us and our brethren who were before us in the faith*" (59:10), other well-known verses with the same import, as well as well-known narrations, such as the Prophet's saying, "O Allah, forgive the people of Baqi al-Gharqad" [i.e. the cemetery of the Companions] and others. There is disagreement among the scholars as to whether the reward of reciting Quran reaches the dead. It is well-known that Shafii and some Shafii scholars said it did not, while Ahmad ibn Hanbal and another group of scholars among whom are Shafiis said that it did reach the dead. It is up to the reciter to say at the end of his recitation: O Allah, bring the reward of what I have recited to So-and-so. And Allah knows best.[53]

Nawawi's words make it patently clear that he did not consider *ihda al-thawab* an innovation; rather, he declared it permissible.

Ibn Taymiyya said, "The sound position is that the deceased gets the benefit of all kinds of bodily worship whether prayer, fasting, or recitation, just as he gets the benefit of acts of monetary worship such as *sadaqa* and its like and just as if one supplicated on his behalf."[54]

Ibn Abi al-Izz al-Hanafi, who adopted the doctrines of Ibn Taymiyya, said, in his commentary on Tahawi's *Aqida*:

> The Sunnis agree that the dead benefit from the striving of the living in two matters: the first is what the dead one himself caused to take place during his life, and the second is the invocation of Muslims on behalf of the dead, their asking forgiveness for them, giving charity, and performing pilgrimage . . .
>
> As for the reward of such bodily worship as fasting, reciting Quran, and *dhikr* reaching the dead, there is disagreement. Abu Hanifa, Ahmad, and the vast majority of the Salaf agree that it reaches the dead, while the more known position of the schools of al-Shafii and Malik is that it does not . . . Some of the innovators among the theologians (*ahl al-kalam* [i.e.

53 Nawawi, *al-Adhkar* (Mecca ed. 1992 p. 208; Taif ed. p. 215 #500).
54 Ibn Taymiyya, *Majmu al-fatawa* (24:300, 24:317).

the Mutazila]) have adduced as proof for the complete lack of benefit for the dead such ambiguous verses as, *"The human being can have nothing but what he strives for"* (53:39), *"Nor are you requited except for what you used to do"* (36:54), and *"For the soul is only what it has earned, and against it only what it has deserved"* (2:286). They also suggest that the established hadith whereby the Prophet (ﷺ) said, "When a human being dies his work ceases, except for three things . . ." shows that the Prophet (ﷺ) said that one only benefits from what one has brought about during his life, and as for the rest then he is cut off from it . . .

But the proof that the dead benefits from other than what he has brought about in his life is in the Book, the *sunna*, consensus, and the sound analogy . . . [After citing several proofs he says.] As for the reaching to the deceased of someone else's reward for fasting, it is narrated in the two *Sahih*s [also Abu Dawud, Ahmad, and al-Nasai] from Aisha that the Prophet (ﷺ) said, "Whoever dies without making up an obligatory fast that he had missed, let his patron (*wali*) fast on his behalf . . ." The Lawgiver pointed, with the reaching of the reward of fasting, to the reaching of the reward for Quranic recitation and other such types of bodily worship. It is made plain by the fact that to fast is merely to restrain the ego from food through intention, and the Lawgiver has prescribed that its reward will reach the dead. What about the reward of recitation which is both work and intention? . . . The recitation of Quran and its voluntary, unpaid donation to the dead do reach him, just as the reward of fasting and pilgrimage reach him.[55]

Mulla Ali al-Qari, in his commentary on Imam Abu Hanifa, said:

> Among them (the rulings that pertain to *barzakh*) is the ruling that the supplications of the living, and the donations on their behalf (*sadaqa*), benefit the dead and raise their positions. This is contrary to the Mutazila, who said that the *qada*, or divine decree, does not change for the dead and that every soul has

---

55 Tahawi, *Aqida*, 1995 ed. 2:664-673.

only what it gained (in life) and cannot acquire what someone else does. The answer to this is that the immutability of *qada* for the dead does not preclude the benefit of the supplication of the living on their behalf, for such benefit may well be part of the *qada* in the first place. Furthermore, it may be that the benefit of the living in supplicating is itself for an action they did in the world and for which they will get the reward in the hereafter.

In addition to all the above, the supplication for the dead is established in sound hadith, especially in *salat al-janaza*. The Salaf transmitted it, and the Khalaf agreed upon it. If there was no benefit in it for the dead it would be in vain; however, many verses of the Quran comprise invocation for the dead, such as, *"O my Lord! Grant them mercy as they raised me when I was young"* (17:24), *"O my Lord! Forgive me and my parents and whomever enters my house a believer, and all believers males and female"* (71:28), *"O our Lord! Forgive us and our brothers who preceded us in faith"* (59:10). It is related from Sad ibn Ubada that he said, "O Messenger of Allah! Umm Sad–in Nasai, my mother–died, what is the best donation (*sadaqa*) [to make on her behalf]?" The Prophet (ﷺ) replied, "Water." Sad dug a well and said, "This is for Umm Sad." Abu Dawud and al-Nasai [with a sound chain] narrated it [also Ibn Majah and Ahmad with a sound chain] . . .

Al-Qunawi said, "The principle inferred from this among Sunnis is that any person can donate the reward of their work to another, whether prayer, fasting, pilgrimage, charity (*sadaqa*), or other than that." Al-Shafii permitted this in charity and acts of monetary worship (*ibada maliyya*), as well as pilgrimage. If someone recites over the grave then the deceased obtains (only) the reward of listening to the Quran, but al-Shafii objected to granting the reward of Quranic recitation to the dead, as well as that of prayer, fasting, and all non-monetary acts of obedience and worship. The position of Abu Hanifa and his companions is that donation is permitted and that the reward (of recitation) does go to the deceased.

Those who object cite the verse, *"The human being can have nothing but what he strives for"* (53:39) and the hadith, "When a human being dies his work ceases, except for three things: an ongoing *sadaqa*, knowledge of his from which people derive benefit, and a righteous child of his who supplicates for him."[56]

The answer is, the verse is a proof for us, because the one who donates the reward of his work to another strives in conveying such reward to the other. Therefore he obtains what he strove for according to that verse, and he does not obtain it except through the reaching of the reward to the one to whom he donates it. Thus the verse is a strong proof for us, not against us! As for the hadith, it indicates that the work of the deceased stops and we hold this to be the case also. However, the issue is only the reaching to him of another's reward. The One who causes the reward to reach the dead is Allah, because the dead do not hear by themselves, and their nearness and distance is all one and the same with relation to Allah's power. He said, *"Call upon Me and I shall respond to you"* (40:60).[57]

Shaykh Muhammad Makhluf said:

As for reciting the Quran for the deceased, whether at his grave or far from it, scholars disagree as to whether the reward for it reaches him. The scholarly majority hold that it does reach him, and this is the truth, especially if the reciter afterwards donates the reward of what he has read to the deceased. In such a case the reciter also receives the reward for his recitation without this diminishing anything from the reward of the deceased.[58]

Shaykh Nuh Ali Salman said:

The position of Hanafis and Hanbalis is that a Muslim is entitled to donate the reward of any kind of worship he performs to whomever he wishes of the Muslim dead. As for Shafiis and Malikis, they distinguish between acts that are valid to perform in anoth-

---

56 Muslim Tirmidhi, and others.
57 Mulla Ali al-Qari, *Sharh al-fiqh al-akbar* (p. 194-197).
   58 *Fatawa shariyya wa buhuth Islamiyya* (2:303). From Nuh Ha Mim Keller's *Reliance of the Traveller* (w35.0).

er's stead and those that are not; the former being valid to donate the reward of to the deceased while the latter are not, though the later scholars of the Shafii and Malikis incline toward the validity of donating the reward of any kind of worship whatsoever to the dead. The Hanafis and Hanbalis adduce the following evidence to support their position:

1 Bukhari and Muslim relate that the Prophet (ﷺ) sacrificed two rams of predominantly white color, one for himself and the other for his Community. The evidence therein is that the Prophet (ﷺ) sacrificed animals and donated the reward to his Community, which includes both the living and the dead, both those who existed in his time and those who came after.

2 Anas relates that he said to the Prophet (ﷺ), "O Messenger of Allah, we give in charity, perform the pilgrimage, and supplicate for our dead. Does this reach them?" He replied, "Yes, indeed it reaches them, and they rejoice thereat just as one of you rejoices at the gift of a tray of food."

3 The Prophet (ﷺ) said, "Whoever dies with an obligatory fast to perform, his responsible family members may fast in his stead."

4 The Prophet (ﷺ) said, "Recite *Ya Sin* [Surah 36 of the Quran] over your dead."

5 Allah Mighty and Majestic has informed us that the angels ask forgiveness for believers, as He says, *"The angels glorify their Lord with praise and ask forgiveness for those on earth"* (42:5). He praises believers who ask forgiveness for their brethren, by saying: *". . . And those who come after them say, 'Lord, forgive us and our brethren who have preceded us in faith'"* (59:10).

6 The Prophet (ﷺ) used to supplicate for those he performed the funeral prayer over. The evidence in all of the above is that supplications are an act of worship, for the Prophet (ﷺ) said, "Supplication is the marrow of worship." The above texts clearly show that supplications benefit others besides the one who makes them, even when the other does not ask for the supplication to be made for him.

The above provides evidence that the deceased benefits from all types of worship, whether monetary or physical, since fasting, pilgrimage, supplications, and asking forgiveness are all physical acts of worship, and Allah Most High conveys the benefit of them to the deceased– and so it must also be with other works."[59]

3.4.3. INSTRUCTING THE DEAD AFTER BURIAL (*TALQIN AL-AMWAT*)

Abu Umama al-Bahili said: Allah's Messenger said:

> When one of you dies and you have settled the earth over him, let one of you stand at the head of his grave and then say, "O so-and-so, son of so-and-so [name of the mother]!," for he will hear you even if he does not reply. Then let one of you say a second time, "O so-and-so, son of so-and-so [name of the mother]!," whereupon he will sit up (in his grave). Then let one of you say, "O so-and-so, son of so-and-so [name of the mother]!" At this the other one will say, "Instruct me, and may Allah grant you mercy!," even if you cannot hear it (*wa lakin la tasmaun*), or [in Ibn Hajar's narration] even if you cannot notice it (*wa lakin la tashurun*). Then let one of you say, "Remember the state in which you left this world, which is your witnessing that there is no god except Allah, and that Muhammad is His Servant and Messenger; that you are pleased with Allah as your Lord, Islam as your religion, Muhammad as your Prophet (ﷺ), and the Quran as your book." At that Munkar and Nakir [the angels of the questioning in the grave] hold each other back, saying, "Let us go; there is no need for us to tarry here, for he has been instructed correctly what to say. [In Tabarani's and Ibn Qudama's narration:] And Allah will accept his argument without the two of them." A man said, "O Messenger of Allah, what if his mother's name is not known?" He replied, "Then let him say, son of Hawwa [Eve]."[60]

---

59 Nuh Ali Salman, *Qada al ibadat wa al-niyaba fiha*, Maktaba al-Risala al-Haditha, Amman, 1403/1983 (p. 400-403). From the *Reliance of the Traveller* (w35.0).

60 It is narrated by Ibn Qudama in *al-Mughni* (1994 ed. 2:319) who mentions that Ibn Shahin narrates it in *Kitab dhikr al-mawt* with his chain. Ibn Hajar in *Talkhis al-kabir* (2:143) said that Tabarani narrates it with an adequate chain *(isnaduhu salih)* which, despite its weakness, is consolidated by the witnessing of sound hadiths, and that Dia al-Din declared it strong *(qawwah)* in his *Ahkam*. Shawkani also narrates it in *Nayl al-awtar* (4:89-90) from the narration of Said in his *Sunan* from Rashid ibn Sad

Among the Hanafis, Ibn Abidin stated that instructing the deceased after burial is lawful, and that it is useful to make him firm and keep him company with a reminder, according to what has been mentioned in the reports.[61]

Nawawi said:

> A very large number of our companions [i.e. of the Shafii school] declared that it is desirable (*mustahabb*) to instruct the deceased after burial. Among those who prescribed it are Qadi Husayn in his *Taliq*, his companion Abu Sad al-Mutawalli in his book *al-Tatimma*, the Shaykh, the Imam, the Zahid Abu al-Fath Nasr ibn Ibrahim ibn Nasr al-Maqdisi, Imam Abu al-Qasim al-Rafii, and others . . . The Shaykh and Imam Abu Amr ibn al-Salah was asked about this instruction to the dead and he said in his *Fatawa*, "The *talqin* is what we choose and what we practice."[62]

Ibn Qudama cites among those who practiced *talqin al-amwat* or declared it desirable, or *mustahabb*:[63]

> Abu al-Mughira
> Abu Bakr ibn Abi Maryam al-Tabii
> Rashid ibn Sad al-Tabii
> Hamza ibn Jundub al-Tabii
> Hakim ibn Umayr al-Tabii
> The shaykhs of the above-named, i.e. among the Companions,
> Ibn Iyash
> Al-Qadi Abu Yala ibn al-Farra
> Abu al-Khattab

and Damara ibn Habib, and he mentions that Abd al-Aziz al-Hanbali also narrated it in his *al-Shafi*. Shawkani's citation of Said's narration is not traced back to the Prophet and its wording is: "They used to like *(kanu yastahibbun)* that it be said to the dead...", "they" referring to the Companions, and Shawkani added that Shafii's companions also considered it *mustahabb* – desirable.

61 Ibn Abidin, *Hashiyat al-durr al-mukhtar*. Hasanayn Muhammad Makhluf mentioned it in his *Fatawa shariyya* (2:272). See also Ibn Abidin's *Shifa al-alil*.
62 Nawawi, *al-Adhkar* (Taif ed. p. 212-213 #494).
63 Ibn Qudama, *al-Mughni* (1994 ed. 2:319).
64 Ibn Qayyim al-Jawziyya, *Kitab al-ruh* (Madani ed. p. 20-21).

Ibn Qayyim al-Jawziyya adds Imam Ahmad to the above list, as stated in the following passage:[64]

Another proof of this [the dead hearing the living] is also the practice of people (*amal al-nas*) formerly and to the present time of instructing the dead in his grave (*talqin al mayyit fi qabrihi*). If the dead did not hear that and did not benefit by it there would be no advantage in it and it would be done in vain. Imam Ahmad was asked about it and he considered it good (*istahsanahu*) and adduced for it a proof from usage (*ihtajja alayhi bi al-amal*).

There is also related on this subject a weak narration that al-Tabarani related in his Mujam from Abu Umama, who said: . . . [see above]. Although this hadith has not been established (*lam yathbut*), the continuity of its practice in every country and time without objection is sufficient warrant for its performance. For Allah certainly never caused a custom (*ada*) to persist so that a people who encompass the eastern and western parts of the earth, and who are the most perfect of peoples in intelligence, and the most comprehensive of them in sciences, should agree to address one who neither hears nor reasons, and approve of that, without some mistrustful one of that people disapproving it! But, the first established it for the last (*sannahu al-awwalu li al-akhir*), and the last imitates the first therein (*wa yaqtadi fihi al-akhiru bi al-awwal*). And were it not that the one who is addressed hears, this act would have the status of address to earth and wood and stone and the non-existent–and this, even if one person might approve of it, the learned would unanimously abhor it and condemn it.

Abu Dawud related in his *Sunan*, with a chain to which there is no objection: The Prophet (※) attended the funeral of a man, and when he was buried he said, "Ask confirmation for your brother, for he is now being questioned." So he gave information that he was being questioned at that time. And since he was being asked, then he could hear the dictation. And it is valid on the Prophet's authority that the dead one hears the beating of their sandals when they turn to leave.

Abd al-Haqq [Ibn al-Kharrat al-Ishbili] related on

the authorities of one of the saints that he said, "A brother of mine died and I saw him in my sleep. I said, 'O brother, what was your state when you were placed in your grave?' He said, 'Someone kept coming to me with a bright flame of fire. If it had not been that someone supplicated for me I would have perished.'"

Shabib ibn Shayba said–he was one of the *tabi al-tabiin*, "My mother enjoined me at her death saying, 'O my son, when you bury me, stand at my grave and say, O mother of Shabib, repeat *la ilaha illallah.*' So when I buried her, I stood at her grave and said, 'O mother of Shabib, repeat *la ilaha illallah.*' Then I departed. When night came, I saw her in my sleep and she said, 'O my son, I was on the point of perishing but for the expression *la ilaha illallah* overtaking me. So you have observed my last wish, O my son.'"

Imam Ahmad's proof from usage, as reported by Ibn Qayyim, conforms with one of the legal bases used by the scholars of *usul* and hadith, and is also the reason why the Shafii master Ibn al-Salah considered *talqin* a *sunna*. This is explained by the hadith master Ibn Hajar:[65]

One of the factors for accepting a hadith [as authentic] to which our shaykh [al-Iraqi] made no objection is the agreement of the scholars on acting upon the prescription of that hadith. This renders it accepted, to the point that acting upon it may be considered required [*wajib*]. This was stated explicitly by a group of the Imams of Legal Principles (*usul*). One example is Imam al-Shafii's statement:

And what I said–that is, concerning the fact that water becomes impure when impurity takes place in it– when the taste of the water or its smell or its color changes, it is narrated from the Prophet (ﷺ) according to a criterion the like of which does not make a narration firmly established among the scholars of hadith. However, it is the saying of the commonality, and I don't know any among them that holds otherwise.

65 Ibn Hajar, *al-Ifsah ala nukat Ibn al-Salah* as quoted by Imam Lucknawi in *al-Ajwiba al-fadila* (p. 231).
66 As reported in *The Reliance of the Traveller* (p. 921-924 w32.1-32.2).

Shaykh Nuh Ali Salman said:[66]

Instructing the deceased (*talqin*) is when a Muslim sits besides the grave of his fellow Muslim after burial to speak to him, reminding him of the Testimony of Faith "There is no god but Allah, Muhammad is the Messenger of Allah," and certain other matters of belief, such as that death is real, paradise is real, hell is real, and that Allah shall raise up those who are in their graves. He also prays that the deceased will prove steadfast when the two angels question him. It does not have a particular form, but rather anything that accomplishes the above is called "instructing the deceased." The following evidence may be adduced for its validity in Sacred Law:

1 The rigorously authenticated (*sahih*) hadith [in Bukhari] that the Prophet (ﷺ) (Allah bless him and give him peace) ordered that the bodies of the idolaters slain on the day of Badr be thrown into a well whose interior was encased with stones. Then he approached the well and began calling the disbelievers by their names and fathers' names, saying, "O so-and-so son of so-and-so, and so-and-so son of so-and-so, it would have been easier if you had obeyed Allah and His Messenger. We have found what our Lord promised to be true; have you found what your Lord promised to be true?" To which Umar said, "O Messenger of Allah, why speak to lifeless bodies?" He replied, "By Him in whose hand is the soul of Muhammad, you do not hear my words better than they do."[67]

2 The Prophet (ﷺ) said, "When a servant is laid in his grave and his friends have turned away from him and he hears the footfalls of their sandals, two angels come to him, sit him upright, and ask him, "What were you wont to say [i.e. what did you use to say] of this man Muhammad (Allah bless him and give him peace)?" The believer will answer, "I testify that he is the slave of Allah and His Messenger," and it will be said, "Look at your place in hell, Allah has changed it for a place in paradise," and the man will behold both of them."

3 Uthman ibn Affan (Allah be well pleased with

---

67 In Muslim it is reported, "By Him in whose hand is the soul of Muhammad, you do not hear my words better than they do, only they are unable to answer."

him) relates that when the Prophet (ﷺ) used to finish burying someone, he would stand by the grave and say, "All of you, ask Allah to forgive your brother and make him steadfast, for he is now being asked."

4 Abu Umama said: When I die, do with me as the Prophet (ﷺ) ordered us, saying, "When one of your brothers die and you have smoothed over the earth upon his grave, let one of you stand at the head of the grave and say, 'O so-and-so son of so-and-so [note: the second "So-and-so" is feminine, naming the deceased's mother]' – for he will hear, though he cannot reply. Then say, 'O so-and-so son of so-and-so,' and he will sit upright. Then say, 'O so-and-so son of so-and-so,' and he will say, 'Direct me, Allah have mercy on you,' though you will not hear it. You should say, 'Remember the creed upon which you departed from this world, the testimony that there is no god but Allah, and Muhammad is His slave and Messenger, and that you accepted Allah as your Lord, Islam as your religion, Muhammad as your Prophet (ﷺ), and the Koran as your exemplar.' For then the two angels Munkar and Nakir will take each other's hand and say, 'Let us go, what is there to keep us beside someone who has been instructed how to make his plea?'" A man said, "O Messenger of Allah, what if one does not know the name of his mother?" and he answered, "Then he should mention his descent from his mother Eve, saying, "O so-and-so son of Eve . . ."

Tabarani related this hadith in his *al-Mujam al-kabir*, and Ibn Hajar Asqalani has said that "its chain of transmission is sound" (*isnaduhu salih*) in *Talkhis al-habir fi takhrij ahadith al-rafii al-kabir* (2:143). Some scholars have said that this hadith is not well authenticated (*daif*), while others have gone to the extreme of calling it a forgery.

The first three of the above hadith, all of them rigorously authenticated (*sahih*), show that:

1 A dead person hears the words of a living person speaking to him and the sounds and movements around him.

2 The dead are questioned in their graves.

3 It is legally valid, after burial, for a living person to ask Allah to forgive the deceased and make him steadfast for the questioning of the two angels.

As for the fourth hadith, scholars have felt comfortable with it (*istanasa bihi al-ulama*), saying that if the deceased can hear, we should let him hear these words which he is in the direst need of in such circumstances, and even if the hadith that has conveyed them is not well authenticated, its content is valid and true (*madmunuhu kalamun haqqun sahih*).

The above is what has been said about instructing the deceased (*talqin*). Whoever does it cannot be blamed, since they have something of a case for it; and whoever does not cannot be blamed, because they do not consider the case sufficient.

4. FASTING AND VOLUNTARY WORSHIP IN THE MONTHS OF RAJAB AND SHABAN

4.1. INTRODUCTION

Questions addressed in this chapter include:

What is the importance of observing the night of the 27th of Rajab (*laylat al-isra* and *miraj*) and the 15th of Shaban (*laylat al-baraa*)?

Is there any evidence from the Quran and hadith that these nights should be held in high esteem, as done by the majority of Muslims who celebrate or commemorate them through gathering, feeding the hungry, reciting Quran and *sira*, reading hadith, performing supererogatory prayers etc.?

What is the exact understanding of the narrations of the Night Journey (*isra*) and Ascension (*miraj*) according to mainstream Islam?

Is there any confirmation or recommendation in the jurisprudence of the major schools about fasting the months of Rajab and Shaban?

What is the position of scholars of the major schools on the permissibility of fasting the three blessed months of Rajab, Shaban, and Ramadan in a row?

4.2. MAINSTREAM ISLAMIC VIEW ON FASTING DURING THE MONTHS OF RAJAB, SHABAN AND THE OTHER HOLY MONTHS

It is recommended to fast the months of Rajab and Shaban as a superogatory worship (*nafil*), with the intention of following the *sunna* of the Prophet (鑾), who has established the merit of this fast. As for extra devotions on certain nights of Rajab and Shaban, such as the night of the Night Journey (*laylat al-isra* 27th of Rajab) and *laylat al-baraa* (15th of Shaban), there are no grounds for prohibiting them.

The following paragraph is a translation of Abd al-Rahman al-Jaziri's chapter entitled "Fasting During Rajab, Shaban, and the Rest of the Holy Months":

> Fasting the months of Rajab and Shaban is recommended (*mandub*) as agreed upon by three of the Imams. The Hanbalis differed in that they said fasting Rajab singly is disliked, except if one breaks the fast during it then it is not disliked. Regarding the holy months, Dhul Qida, Dhul Hijja, Muharram, and Rajab, fasting them is recommended according to three of the Imams. The Hanafis differed in that they said that what is recommended in the Holy months is to fast three days from each of them, which are Thursday, Friday and Saturday.[1]

4.3. HADITH ON FASTING DURING THE MONTH OF RAJAB

1 Uthman ibn Hakim al-Ansari said: I asked Said ibn Jubayr about fasting in Rajab, and we were then passing through the month of Rajab, whereupon he said:

> I heard Ibn Abbas saying, "The Messenger of Allah used to observe fast so continuously that we thought he would never break it, and at other times he remained without fasting so continuously that we thought he would never fast."[2]

---

1 Al-Jaziri, *al-Fiqh ala al-madhahib al-arbaa* (Islamic law according to the Four Schools) (Beirut: Dar al-fikr) 1:557.

2 Muslim and Abu Dawud relate it in *Kitab al-sawm*, respectively in the chapter on fasting at times other than Ramadan, and in the chapter of fasting during Rajab, also Ahmad in his *Musnad*.

Imam Nawawi commented on this saying:

> It appears that the meaning inferred by Said ibn
> Jubayr from Ibn Abbas' report is that fasting in Rajab
> is neither forbidden nor considered praiseworthy in
> itself. Rather, the ruling concerning it is the same as
> the rest of the months.[3]
> Neither prohibition nor praiseworthiness has
> been established for the month of Rajab in itself.
> However, the principle concerning fasting is that it is
> praiseworthy in itself, and in the *Sunan of Abu
> Dawud*[4] the Prophet (囲) has made the fasting of the
> sacred months praiseworthy, and Rajab is one of
> them. And Allah knows best.[5]

It is established, on the one hand, that Ibn Umar fasted
during the sacred months,[6] and on the other, that he fasted all
year as shown by the following hadith.

2 Abd Allah, the freed slave of Asma the daughter of Abu
Bakr, the maternal uncle of the son of Ata, reported:

> Asma sent me to Abdullah ibn Umar saying, "The
> news has reached me that you prohibit the use of
> three things: the striped robe, saddle-cloth made of
> red silk, and fasting the whole month of Rajab."
> Abdullah said to me, "So far as what you say about
> fasting in the month of Rajab, how about one who
> observes continuous fasting? And so far as what you
> say about the striped garment, I heard Umar ibn al-
> Khattab say that he had heard from Allah's
> Messenger, 'He who wears a silk garment, has no
> share for him (in the hereafter).'" And I am afraid that
> stripes were part of it. And so far as the red saddle
> cloth is concerned, here is my saddle cloth and it is
> red." I went back to Asma and informed her, so she
> said, "Here is the cloak (*jubba*) of Allah's Messenger."
> She brought to me a cloak made of Persian cloth with
> a hem of (silk) brocade, and its sleeves bordered with

---

3 This is also the commentary of Qastallani in *al-Mawahib al-laduniyya* (Beirut,
1996) 3:301.

4 Abu Dawud, *Sunan, Kitab al-siyam*, Chapter: "Fasting During the Sacred
Months." Also in Ibn Majah and Ahmad, hadith of the man who repeats: "I can bear
more," and to whom the Prophet finally says: "Fast during the sacred months."

5 Nawawi, *Sharh sahih Muslim, Kitab* 13 *Bab* 34 #179.

6 *Musannaf Abd al-Razzaq* 4:293, *Musannaf Ibn Abi Shayba* 1:125.

(silk) brocade, and said, "This was Allah's Messenger's cloak with Aisha until she died, then I took possession of it. The Apostle of Allah used to wear that, and we washed it for the sick so that they could seek healing with it."[7]

Nawawi commented:

> Ibn Umar's reply concerning fasting in Rajab is a denial on his part of what Asma had heard with regard to his forbidding it, and it is an affirmation that he fasted Rajab in its entirety as well as fasting permanently, i.e. except the days of *id* and *tashriq*.[8] This (perpetual fast) is his way, the way of his father Umar ibn al-Khattab, Aisha, Abu Talha, and others of the Salaf as well as Shafii and other scholars. Their position is that perpetual fasting is not disliked (*makruh*).

Ibn Qudama states something similar concerning perpetual fasting. He adds that the same view is related from Ahmad and Malik, and that after the Prophet's death Abu Talha fasted permanently for forty years, among other Companions.[8] Also, Ibn Hajar al-Haytami relates that Abu Hanifa was never seen eating except at night.[9]

Nawawi adds:

> In this hadith is a proof that it is recommended to seek blessings through the relics of the righteous and their clothes (*wa fi hadha al-hadith dalil ala istihbab al-tabarruk bi athar al-salihin wa thiyabihim*).[10]

Bayhaqi relates in *Shuab al-iman* and Abu Nuaym in *al-Targhib*:

> Abu Abd Allah al-Hafiz (this is al-Hakim) and
> Abu Muhammad ibn Abi Hamid al-Muqri said:
> from Abu al-Abbas al-Asamm,

---

7 Muslim relates it in the first chapter of *Kitab al-libas*, and Ibn Majah in the book of Fasting.

8 *Ayyam al-tashriq* are the Days of drying the meat after the sacrifice of *Id al-Adha* = 11, 12, and 13 of Dhu al-hijja.

9 Ibn Qudama, *al-Mughni* (Beirut, 1414/1994 ed.) 3:119.

10 Al-Haytami, *al-Khayrat al-hisan fi manaqib Abi Hanifa al-Numan* (Cairo: al-Halabi, 1326) p. 40.

from Ibrahim ibn Sulayman al-Barlisi,
from Abdallah ibn Yusuf,
from Amir ibn Shibli who said:
I heard Abu Qilaba say, "There is a palace in
paradise for those who fast the month of
Rajab."[11]

Bayhaqi comments:

Even if it is *mawquf* at Abu Qilaba (i.e. not traced
back to the Prophet (ﷺ)), who is one of the Successors
(d. 104), such as he does not say such a saying except
if it were related to him by someone who had heard it
from him to whom revelation comes (i.e. the Prophet
(ﷺ)), and success is from Allah.[12]

4.3.1. INCORRECT "SALAFI" OBJECTIONS TO FASTING DURING THE HOLY MONTHS

Those who object to fasting part or all of Rajab and Shaban
cite the following:

1 Umar's punishment of the *mutarajjibun*, those who fasted the month of Rajab according to a practice carried over from
the Age of Ignorance (*jahiliyya*), by striking their hands until
they broke their fast.

However, this does not constitute a valid objection, as
Umar's act was based solely on the undue emphasis by some
people on Rajab. Rajab used to be fasted during the Age of
Ignorance (*jahiliyya*), over Ramadan as the fasting month. This
is clearly not the case for present-day Muslims. There was also
a sacrifice named *rajabiyya* performed in that month, which
was a practice carried over from the Age of Ignorance
(*jahiliyya*). Several hadith in Abu Dawud and Ahmad show that
it became obligatory in Islam until the obligation was abrogated. Certain pre-Islamic remnants were fought even in the time
of Umar, as is shown by the latter's uprooting of a tree for fear
of its veneration by some people.

It must be understood that Umar never said, "Don't fast."
Rather, he said, "Break your fast," meaning "do not complete it

---

11 Nawawi, *Sharh sahih Muslim Kitab* 37 *Bab* 2 #10.
12 Bayhaqi, *Shuab al-iman* 3:368 #3802; Abu Nuaym, *al-Targhib* #1821.

as you would be obliged to if it were Ramadan." No one fasted Rajab and Shaban completely, as this was reserved for Ramadan. However, if someone makes the intention to fast Rajab and Shaban completely, it is permitted in the Sharia, with the understanding that it is *mustahabb* to break it shortly before Ramadan begins.

Ibn Qudama states in *al-Mughni*:

> It is disliked that Rajab be singled out for fasting. Ahmad said, "If a man fasts during that month, let him break the fast for one day in it, or several, just so as not to fast it all."

The reason for this is what Ahmad has narrated with his chains:

> From Kharasha ibn al-Hurr: I saw Umar striking the hands of the *mutarajjibin* until they helped themselves to the food, and he would say, "Eat! For it is only a month which the Age of Ignorance (jahiliyya) used to magnify."

> From Abd Allah ibn Umar that he would dislike to see the people make preparations for Rajab and would say, "Fast some of it and break fast some of it."

> From Ibn Abbas, something similar.

> From Abu Bakrah: He saw his household preparing new baskets and clay jugs and said, "What is this?" They said, "For Rajab, so that we may fast it." He said, "Did you change Rajab into Ramadan?" Then he took apart the baskets and broke the jugs.

> And Imam Ahmad said, "Whoever fasts all year round may fast all of Rajab. Otherwise, let him not fast all of it but only some of it so that he will not liken it to Ramadan."[13]

The above makes it clear that:
• Singling out the month of Rajab for fasting is not forbidden, but is, at worst, disliked

13 Ibn Qudama, *al-Mughni* 3:118-119.

• It is not even disliked, as long as one's fast is broken so as to disassociate this fast from the month of Ramadan
• Even unbroken fast is not disliked if the person fasts all year round

2 Others cite Sayyid Sabiq's statement in *Fiqh as-sunnah*:

> Fasting during Rajab contains no more virtue than during any other month. There is no sound report from the *sunna* that states that it has a special reward. All that has been related concerning it is not strong enough to be used as a proof. Ibn Hajar says, "There is no authentic hadith related to its virtues, nor fasting during it or on certain days of it, nor concerning exclusively making night prayers during that month."[14]

The opinion of Sayyid Sabiq, that "Fasting during Rajab contains no more virtue than during any other month . . ," is certainly incorrect in view of the fact that Rajab is a sacred month, and the Prophet (ﷺ) emphasized the merit of fasting in the sacred months, and in Shaban. This is established by Nawawi's commentary on the hadith of Said ibn Jubayr, as well as the following hadiths:

1 From Mujiba al-Bahiliyya who reported that her father or uncle was told by the Prophet (ﷺ) three times, "Fast some and leave some in the sacred months."[15]
2 From Usama ibn Zayd, "O Messenger of Allah . . . I never saw you fast any month (besides Ramadan) as much as you fast during the month of Shaban." He said, "The people become inattentive during that month between Rajab and Ramadan (i.e. between two great months), and it is a month in which actions are raised to the Lord of the worlds, therefore I like that my actions be raised while I am fasting."[16]

---

14 Sayyid Sabiq, *Fiqh as-sunnah*, Alms tax and Fasting, trans. Muhammad Saeed Dabas and Jamal al-Din M. Zarabozo (ATP, 1989) p. 127-128.

15 Abu Dawud, *Siyam* Chapter 54; Bayhaqi, *al-Sunan al-kubra* 4:291; Suyuti, *al-Durr al-manthur* 3:235.

16 Ahmad, *Musnad* 5:201.

3 From Aisha, "The Prophet (ﷺ) used to fast the whole of Shaban but for a little."[17]

From Abu Hurayra, the Prophet (ﷺ) said, "The best month to fast after Ramadan is Muharram."[18]

As for the *hafiz* Ibn Hajar's opinion that fasting during Rajab contains no particular virtue–assuming it is correctly related from him–it only applies to the singling out of the month of Rajab and the exclusion of Ramadan, Shaban, the sacred months, or the rest of the year, because there is no basis for singling out these cases. His opinion, therefore, does not provide a basis for the objectors' claim that fasting during Rajab is forbidden, or that it is an innovation; neither the Imams of the fours schools, Bayhaqi, Nawawi, Ibn Hajar, nor Sayyid Sabiq have claimed this. Furthermore, there is also no sound hadith from the Prophet (ﷺ) forbidding the fast of Rajab or disavowing its merit.

> 3 As for those who object by quoting the hadith whereby the Prophet (ﷺ) emphasized that the one who fasts all his life has not fasted,[19] their understanding of this hadith is diametrically opposed to that of the Companions and the Salaf, Abu Hanifa, Malik, Shafii, and Ahmad. They did not dislike perpetual fasting as long as it did not include the days of *id* and *tashriq*.
> 4 As for the narration from Ibn Abbas, whereby the Prophet (ﷺ) forbade the fast of Rajab, only Ibn Majah reports it. His chain contains Dawud ibn Ata al-Muzani, about whom Bukhari, Ibn Abi Hatim, and Abu Zura said, "His hadith is rejected" (*munkar al-hadith*). Nisai declared him *daif*, and Ahmad said, "He is nothing." The chain also contains Abu Ayyub Sulayman ibn Ali al-Hashimi about whom Yahya ibn Said al-Qattan said: "His case is not known," although Ibn Hibban declared him trustworthy, but Ibn Hibban's leniency in this is known.
> 5 As for the hadith in Tirmidhi, Ahmad, Abu Dawud, and Darimi concerning the Prophet's injunction to refrain from fasting in the second half of

17 In Bukhari and Muslim.
18 In Muslim
19 In Bukhari and Muslim.

Shaban, it applies to those who would deliberately intend to fast only then, as Tirmidhi explained. It should not be done in view of the proximity of the month of Ramadan. As for those who were fasting before, then they may fast in the second half of Shaban.

In conclusion, it is at the very least allowed to fast Rajab and Shaban in part or in whole. It is recommended, as the intention to follow the *sunna* and the knowledge that only the fast of Ramadan is obligatory preclude the reprehensibility of those who used to favor Rajab instead of Ramadan. Sufficient proof that the month of Rajab is a great month lies in the fact that it is the month of the Prophet's rapture and ascension to his Lord (*al-isra wa al-miraj*).[20]

4.4. COMMEMORATING THE PROPHET'S NIGHT JOURNEY (*ISRA* AND *MIRAJ*) ON THE 27TH OF RAJAB[21]

The following section is a compilation of the hadith on *al-isra wa al-miraj* by Muhammad Alawi Maliki of Makka.

The Shaykh of Makka–may Allah grant him long life and health–Sayyid Muhammad Alawi al-Maliki al-Hasani composed an excellent booklet entitled *al-Anwar al-bahiyya min isra wa miraj khayr al-bariyya* (The resplendent lights of the rapture and ascension of the best of creation). This booklet is of such importance to the subject that it is translated here in its entirety.[22]

I.

Praise be to Allah Who has chosen His praiseworthy servant Muhammad to carry the Message, distinguished him with the sudden rapture on the Buraq

---

20 There is also an early Shii scholar named Muhammad ibn Ali ibn Babawayh al-Qummi (d. 380) who wrote *Fadail al-ashhur al-thalatha: 1. Shahr Rajab, 2. Shahr Shaban, 3. Shahr Ramadan* (Najaf: Matbaat al-adab, 1396/1976). Neither this volume nor *hafiz* al-Kattani's book on the merits of Rajab were available to us.

21 Sayyid Muhammad Alawi al-Maliki al-Hasani, *al-Anwar al-bahiyya min isra wa miraj khayr al-bariyya* (The resplendent lights of the rapture and ascension of the best of creation). (Makka: s.n., 1414/1993).

22 *Ibid.*

(lightning-mount), and caused him to ascend on the ladders of perfection to the high heavens to show him of the greatest signs of his Lord. He raised him until he reached to the Lote-tree of the Farthest Boundary where ends the science of every Messenger-Prophet (鬱) and every Angel Brought Near; where lies the Garden of Retreat, to the point where he heard the sound of the pens that write what befell and what is to befall.

There He manifested Himself to him through vision and addressed him intimately in the station of encounter, accompanying him so that he was no longer alone. There He stilled his fear in those lofty worlds and He communicated to him what He wished, and revealed to him what He wished, and taught him what He wished, and explained to him what He wished. He showed him of the signs of sovereignty and the signs of creation and of the unseen that point to the uniqueness and perfection of His immense majesty, and the marvels of His lordly power, and the sublimity of His wisdom without beginning. Glory to Him, the God that knows the heart's secret and its confidence, and knows what is more subtle and more hidden! He hears the patter of the black ant's feet on a massive rock in the dark night.

I bear witness that there is no god but Allah, Who is sanctified in His essence from all figural representation and shades, and elevated above having a partner in His attributes and acts. I bear witness that our master Muhammad is His servant and Messenger, whose rank He has raised so that none of the seven skies can reach it, nor any of the prophets. For how could they reach his stature when they were shown to him in the Sanctified House in Jerusalem, where Gabriel gave him precedence over them so that he led them in prayer, then apprised him of their places and stations in the heavens, showing that he has been their paramount chief and foremost leader since the beginning?

Allah bore witness that the Prophet (鬱) was the Guide through his knowledge and the Just Instructor in his actions. He elevated his speaking manner above vanity and disgrace; He freed his innermost being from belying what his eyes saw; and He kept his eyes from falsehood and transgression. Then he saw his Lord in the station of proximity and servant-hood. Nor did he fall short of uncovering the reality of the event, but he received all that was communicated to him of both partial and total knowledge.

May Allah's blessing and peace be upon him and upon his Family, the People of Guidance and Firmness, and upon his excellent and pure Companions, carriers of the burdens of the prophetic inheritance, defenders of the precious religion with every burnished sword, who have triumphed and won the highest dwellings of the Abode of Eternity.

To begin, the indigent in need of the mercy of his generous Lord, Muhammad ibn Alawi ibn Abbas al-Maliki al-Hasani says– may Allah treat him with His radiant kindness, "Allah has granted me the favor of writing a vast treatise covering the substantial research which has been done on the subject of *al-isra* and *al-miraj*. Then He expanded my breast so that I could gather its account into a single text as a sepa-rate monograph so as to allow its access to the people at large." In this way they can familiarize themselves with that text and recite it in the public meetings and great celebrations in which Muslims gather to com-memorate *al-isra wa al-miraj*, as is the custom in many countries, especially in the two Holy Sanctuaries.

I have collated my own work with that of the *hafiz* al-Shami and Najm al-Din al-Ghayti to make a single comprehensive text with the mention of additions in their appropriate places. This text includes most of the different narrations on this subject. I have pro-vided a concise commentary and brief notes explain-ing the meaning of rare or difficult words. I have named this treatise, *al-Anwar al-bahiyya min isra wa miraj khayr al-bariyya*, (The resplendent lights of the rapture and ascension of the best of creation),' asking Allah to grant benefit with it and accept it as purely for His sake. Allah's blessings and peace be upon our master Muhammad and his Family and Companions.

II.

The striving of the scholars in organizing

the account of *isra* and *miraj* into a single version

Islamic scholars have organized the accounts of the Prophet's *isra* and *miraj* and gathered its narrations into a single version, while mentioning the various additions, in order to facilitate its perusal and its benefit. In this way they gathered the narrations in one place for the people at large. This is permitted according to the stated rules of the experts in the field of hadith. Many of these experts have used this method in many instances, joining together several narrations of a single event as was done with the Farewell Pilgrimage and some of the military raids and campaigns. The hadith master al-Shami did this with the account of the Prophet's rapture and Ascension, as did the hadith master al-Ghayti[23] and a number of other scholars. This is what al-Shami said on the question of gathering narrations in his great book *al-Miraj*:

Know—may Allah have mercy on you and I—that each of the hadith of the Companions [on this subject] contains what the other does not. Therefore I consulted Allah Almighty and compiled them, rearranging the account into a single text so that it would be sweeter to attentive ears, and in order for its benefit to suit all occasions.

If someone says, 'Each hadith of the *miraj* differs from the next and the ascension may number according to the number of their accounts. Why then did you make all of them into a single account?' I respond, 'The author of *Zad al-maad* [Ibn al-Qayyim] said: "This is the path of the feeble-minded among the literalists of the Zahiri school who are authorities in transmitted texts. If they see in the account a wording that differs from the version of one of the narrators they multiply the occurrence of the event accordingly. The correct view is what the Imams of text transmission have said; namely, that the *miraj* took place once, in Makka, after the beginning of prophethood. It is a wonder how these have claimed that it took place repeatedly. How can they countenance the conclusion that every time, fifty prayers are prescribed upon him then he goes back and forth between Musa and his

---

23 Muhammad ibn Ahmad al-Ghayti (d. 984), *Mawsuat al-isra wa al-miraj al-musamma tatriz al-dibaj bi haqaiq al-isra wa al-miraj* (Beirut: Dar wa-maktaba al-Hilal, 1994).

Lord until they become five. His Lord says:,"I have decreed what is due Me and have reduced the burden of My slaves," only for him to come a second time with fifty prayers which he decreases again, ten by ten?

The hadith master Imad al-Din Ibn Kathir said in his history [*al-Bidaya wa al-nihaya*], after noting that Malik ibn Sasaa's version did not mention Jerusalem:

Some of the narrators would omit part of the report due to its being known, or due to forgetfulness, or because he would mention only what he considered important, or because one time he would feel eager to relate it completely, while another time he would tell his public what is of most use to them.

He who relates every differing narration to a separate occurrence thereby affirming several ascension has strayed widely and said something indefensible and has not fulfilled his pursuit. The reason is that all of the versions contain his meeting with the prophets and the prescription of the prayers upon him; how then could one defend multiplying these occurrences? This understanding is extremely far-fetched nor was it related from any of the Salaf, whereas if this had indeed taken place several times the Prophet (ﷺ) would have reported it to his Community and the people would have transmitted it often.[24]

III.
The Collated Hadith of *isra* and *miraj*
In the name of Allah
Most Merciful Most Beneficent
Blessings and Peace upon the Messenger of Allah,
  his Family, and his Companions

As the Prophet (ﷺ) was in *al-Hijr* at the House

---

24 The author holds that the night ascension of the Prophet to his Lord were numerous. Some of the evidence for this is in the hadith whereby he said: "My eyes sleep but my heart does not sleep."(Bukhari and Muslim). "I have a time with my Lord which no Angel-Brought-Near nor Messenger-Prophet shares with me." Al-Qari commented on this hadith: It is inferred from it that what he means by the angel brought near is Gabriel, while the Messenger-Prophet is his brother the Friend of Allah [Abraham]. Reflect upon this. This hadith also points to the station of self-immersion in the meeting expressed in terms of intoxication, self-effacement, and self-annihilation. Al-Ajluni in *Kashf al-khafa* (2:244) and al-Qari in *al-Asrar al-marfua* (p. 199) said that the hadith master al-Damyati said that al-Khatib narrated it with a chain that meets the criteria of soundness).

(the semi-circular space under the waterspout that is open on both sides on the Northwest side of the Kabah), lying down at rest between two men (his uncle Hamza and his cousin Jafar ibn Abi Talib), Gabriel and Michael came to him. With them was a third angel (Israfil). They carried him until they reached the spring of Zamzam, where they asked him to lie on his back and Gabriel took him over from the other two. (Another version says:) 'The roof of my house was opened and Gabriel descended.'

He split the Prophet's chest from his throat to the bottom of his belly. Then Gabriel said to Michael, 'Bring me a *tast* (a vessel, usually made of copper) of water from Zamzam so that I will purify his heart and expand his breast.' He took out his heart and washed it three times, removing from it what was wrong. Michael went back and forth to him with the vessel of water from Zamzam three times.

Then he brought him a golden vessel filled with wisdom and belief that he emptied into his chest. He filled his chest with *hilm* (intelligence, patience, good character), knowledge, certainty, and submission, then he closed it up. He sealed it between his shoulders with the seal of prophethood.

Then he brought the Buraq, handsome-faced and bridled, a tall, white beast, bigger than the donkey but smaller than the mule. He could place his hooves at the farthest boundary of his gaze. He had long ears. Whenever he faced a mountain his hind legs would extend, and whenever he went downhill his front legs would extend. He had two wings on his thighs that lent strength to his legs.

He bucked when the Prophet (ﷺ) came to mount him. Gabriel put his hand on his mane and said, "Are you not ashamed, O Buraq? By Allah, no one has ridden you in all creation more dear to Allah than he is." Hearing this he was so ashamed that he sweated until he became soaked, and he stood still so that the Prophet (ﷺ) mounted him.

The other prophets used to mount the Buraq before. Said ibn al-Musayyib said, 'It is the beast of Abraham (ﷺ) which he used to mount whenever he travelled to the Sacred House.'

Gabriel departed with him. He placed himself on his right while Michael was on his left. (In Ibn Sad's version:) The one holding his stirrup was Gabriel and the one holding the reins of the Buraq was Michael.

They traveled until they reached a land filled with datepalms. Gabriel said to the Prophet (☫), 'Alight and pray here.' He did so and remounted, then Gabriel said, 'Do you know where you prayed?' He said no. Gabriel said, 'You prayed in a *tayba* (land of pastures) and the Migration will take place there.'

The Buraq continued his lightning flight, placing his hooves wherever his gaze could reach. Gabriel then said again, 'Alight and pray here.' He did so and remounted, then Gabriel said, 'Do you know where you prayed?' He said no. Gabriel said, 'You prayed in Madyan (a city on the shore of the Red Sea bordering Tabuk near the valley of Shuayb) at the tree of Moses" (where Moses rested from fatigue and hunger during his flight from Pharaoh).'

The Buraq continued his lightning flight, then Gabriel said again, 'Alight and pray here.' He did so and remounted, then Gabriel said, 'Do you know where you prayed?' He said no. Gabriel said, 'You prayed at the mountain of Sina (Mount Sinai) where Allah addressed Moses.'

Then he reached a land where the palaces of Syria became visible to him. Gabriel said to him, 'Alight and pray.' He did so and remounted, then the Buraq continued his lightning flight and Gabriel said, 'Do you know where you prayed?' He said no. Gabriel said, 'You prayed in Bethlehem (Bayt Lahm), where Jesus son of Mary was born.'

As the Prophet (☫) was traveling mounted on the Buraq he saw a devil from the *jinn* who was trying to get near him holding a firebrand. Everywhere the Prophet (☫) turned he would see him. Gabriel said to him, 'Shall I teach you words which, if you say them, his firebrand will go out and he will fall dead?' The Prophet (☫) said yes. Gabriel said: Say: *audhu bi wajhillahi al-karim wa bi kalimatillahi al-tammat al-lati la yujawizuhunna barrun wa la fajir min shar-ri ma yanzilu min al-sama wa min sharri ma yaruju fiha wa min sharri ma dharaa fi al-ard wa min shar-*

ri ma yakhruju minha wa min fitani al-layli wa al-nahar wa min tawariq al-layli wa al-nahar illa tariqin yatruqu bi khayrin ya rahman (I seek refuge in the Face of Allah the Munificent and in Allah's perfect words which neither the righteous nor the disobedient overstep from the evil of what descends from the heaven and the evil of what ascends to it and the evil of what is created in the earth and the trials of the night and the day and the visitors of the night and the day except the visitor that comes with goodness, O Beneficent One!). At this the devil fell dead on his face and his firebrand went out.

They traveled until they reached a people who sowed in a day and reaped in a day. Every time they reaped, their harvest would be replenished as before. The Prophet (ﷺ) said, 'O Gabriel, what is this?' He replied, "These are *al-mujahidun* (those who strive) in the path of Allah the Exalted. Every good deed of theirs is multiplied for them seven hundred times, and whatever they spend returns multiplied.'

The Prophet (ﷺ) then noticed a fragrant wind and said, 'O Gabriel, what is this sweet scent?' He replied, 'This is the scent of the lady who combed the hair of Pharaoh's daughter and that of her children. As she combed the hair of Pharaoh's daughter the comb fell and she said, *'Bismillah taisa firawn* (in the name of Allah, may Pharaoh perish!)' Whereupon Pharaoh's daughter said, 'Do you have a Lord other than my father?' She said yes. Pharaoh's daughter said, 'Shall I tell my father?' She said yes. She told him and he summoned the woman and said, 'Do you have a Lord other than me?' She replied, 'Yes, my Lord and your Lord is Allah."

This woman had two sons and a husband. Pharaoh summoned them and he began to entice the woman and her husband to give up their religion, but they refused. He said, 'Then I shall kill you.' She said, 'Be so good as to bury us all together in a single grave if you kill us.' He replied, 'Granted, and it is your right to ask us.' He then ordered that a huge cow made of copper be filled with boiling liquid (oil and water) and that she and her children be thrown into it. The children were taken and thrown in one after the other.

The second and youngest was still an infant at the breast. When they took him he said, 'Mother! fall and do not tarry for verily you are on the right.' Then she was thrown in with her children."

He (Ibn Abbas) said, 'Four spoke from the cradle as they were still infants: this child, Joseph's witness (cf. 12:26), Jurayj's companion, and Jesus son of Mary.'[25]

Then the Prophet (ﷺ) saw people whose heads were being shattered, then every time they would return to their original state and be shattered again without delay. He asked, 'O Gabriel, who are these people?' He replied, 'These are the people whose heads were too heavy (on their pillows) to get up and fulfill the prescribed prayers.'

Then he saw a people who wore loincloths on the fronts and on their backs. They were roaming the way camels and sheep roam about. They were eating this-tles and *zaqqum* –the fruit of a tree that grows in hell and whose fruit resembles the head of devils (37:62-63)–and white-hot coals and stones of hell. He asked, 'Who are these people, O Gabriel?' He replied, 'These are the ones who did not meet the obligation of pay-ing charity from what they possessed, whereas Allah never kept anything from them.'

Then he saw a people who had in front of them excellent meats disposed in pots and also putrid, foul meat, and they would eat from the foul meat and not touch the good meat. He asked, 'What is this, O Gabriel?' He replied, 'These are the men from your Community who had an excellent, lawful wife at home and who would go and see a foul woman and spend the night with her; and the women who would leave their excellent, lawful husband to go and see a foul man and spend the night with him.'

Then he came to a plank in the middle of the road which not even a piece of cloth nor less than that could cross except it would be pierced. He asked,

---

25 Ibn Hajar mentions that the account of the lady who combed the hair of Pharaoh's daughter is narrated from Ibn Abbas by Ahmad, al-Hakim, Ibn Hibban, and al-Bazzar, while Muslim in *Kitab al-zuhd wa al-raqaiq* (#3005) mentions the part of the infant speaking to his mother before they are both thrown into the fire, and the mention of Yusuf's witness in verse 12:26 as being an infant is narrated from Ibn Abbas by Ibn Abi Hatim with a weak chain, and it is held by al-Hasan al-Basri and Said ibn Jubayr. [It is also the explanation retained by Suyuti in *Tafsir al-jalalayn*.] This brings the number of speaking infants alluded to in the hadith "Those who spoke from the cra-dle are three" (Bukhari, Muslim, Ahmad) up to five, and there are reports that increase it to seven or more. Allah knows best. Ibn Hajar, *Fath al-Bari* (1989 ed.) 6:593-594.

'What is this, O Gabriel?' He replied, 'This is what happens to those of your Community who sit in the middle of the road and cut it' and he recited: '*Wa la taqadu bi kulli siratin tuiduna wa tasudduna an sabilillah man amana bihi wa tabtaghunaha iwajan* (*lurk not on every road to threaten wayfarers and to turn away from Allah's path him who believes in Him, and to seek to make it crooked*)' (7:86).

The Prophet (ﷺ) saw a man swimming in a river of blood and he was being struck in his mouth with rocks that he then swallowed. The Prophet (ﷺ) asked, 'What is this, O Gabriel?' He replied, 'This is what happens to those who eat usury.'

Then he saw a man who had gathered a stack of wood that he could not carry, yet he was adding more wood to it. He asked, 'What is this, O Gabriel?' He replied, 'This is a man from your Community who gets people's trusts when he cannot fulfill them, yet he insists on carrying them.'

He then saw people whose tongues and lips were being sliced with metal knives. Every time they were sliced they would return to their original state to be sliced again without respite. He asked, 'Who are these, O Gabriel?' Gabriel replied, 'These are the public speakers of division in your Community; they say what they don't do.'

Then he passed by people who had copper nails with which they scratched their own faces and chests. He asked, 'Who are these, O Gabriel?' Gabriel replied, 'These are the ones who ate the flesh of people and tarnished their reputations.'

Then he saw a small hole with a huge bull coming out of it. The bull began to try entering the hole again and was unable. The Prophet (ﷺ) asked, 'What is this, O Gabriel?' Gabriel replied, 'This is the one in your Community who tells an enormity, then he feels remorse to have spoken it but is unable to take it back.'

(Al-Shami added:) He then came to a valley in which he breathed a sweet, cool breeze fragrant with musk and he heard a voice. He asked, 'What is this, O Gabriel?' Gabriel replied, 'This is the voice of paradise saying: "O my Lord, bring me what You have promised me for too abundant are my rooms, my gold-laced garments, my silk, my brocades, my carpets, my pearls, my coral, my silver, my gold, my goblets, my bowls, my pitchers, my couches, my honey, my water, my milk, my wine!"'

And He says: 'You will have every single male and female Muslim, and every believing Muslim male and female, and everyone who has believed in Me and My Messengers and did excellent deeds without associating a partner to Me nor taking helpers without Me. Anyone who fears Me will be safe, and whoever asks Me I shall give him, and whoever lends Me something I shall repay him, and whoever relies on Me I shall suffice him. I am Allah besides Whom there is no god. I never fail in My promise. Successful indeed are the believers! Blessed is Allah, therefore, the best of Creators!'

And paradise answered, 'I accept.'

Then he came to a valley in which he heard a detestable sound and smelled a stench-carrying wind. He asked, 'What is this, O Gabriel?' Gabriel replied, "This is the sound of hell saying: "O Lord, give me what You promised me, for abundant are my chains, my yokes, my punishments, my fires, my thistles, my pus, my tortures! My depth is abysmal, my heat is extreme, therefore give me what You promised me!"'

And He replied, 'You will have every idolater and idolatress, every male and female disbeliever and foul one, and every tyrant who does not believe in the Day of Reckoning.'

The Prophet (ﷺ) saw the Dajjal in his actual likeness. He saw him with his own eyes, not in a dream. It was said to him, 'O Messenger of Allah, how was he when you saw him?' He replied, 'Mammoth-sized (*faylamaniyyan*), extremely pale and white (*aqmaru hijan*), one of his eyes is protuberant as if it were a twinkling star. His hair is like the branches of a tree. He resembles Abd al-Uzza ibn Qatan (who died in the Age of Ignorance).'

The Prophet (ﷺ) saw a pearl-like white column (*amud*) which the angels were carrying. He asked, 'What is this you are carrying?' They replied,'The

Column of Islam. We have been ordered to place it in Syria' (end of al-Shami's addition).[26]

As the Prophet (ﷺ) was traveling he heard someone calling him from his right, 'O Muhammad, look at me, I want to ask you something!' But the Prophet (ﷺ) did not respond. Then he asked, 'Who was that, O Gabriel?' He replied, 'That is the herald of the Jews. If

[26] (1) The Prophet called Sham (Damascus and Syria) the purest of Allah's lands, the place where Religion, belief and safety are found in the time of dissension, and the home of the saints for whose sake Allah sends sustenance to the people and victory to Muslims over their enemies:1. Ibn Asakir in *Tahdhib tarikh Dimashq al-kabir* relates from Ibn Masud that the Prophet compared the world to a little rain water on a mountain plateau of which the *safw* had already been drunk and from which only the *kadar* or dregs remained. al-Huwjiri and al-Qushayri mention it in their chapters on *tasawwuf*, respectively in *Kashf al-mahjub* and *al-Risala al-qushayriyya*. Ibn al-Athir defines *safw* and *safwa* in his dictionary *al-Nihaya* as "the best of any matter, its quintessence, and purest part." The quintessence spoken of by the Prophet is Sham, because he called Sham "the quintessence of Allah's lands" *(safwat Allah min biladih)*. Tabarani related it from Irbad ibn Sariya and Haythami authenticated the chain of transmission in his book *Majma al-zawaid,* chapter entitled *Bab fadail al-sham.*

(2) Abu al-Darda narrated that the Prophet said: As I was sleeping I saw the Column of the Book being carried away from under my head. I feared lest it would be taken away, so I followed it with my eyes and saw that it was being planted in Sham. Verily, in the time of dissensions, belief will be in Sham. Al-Haythami said that Ahmad narrated it with a chain whose narrators are all the men of the *sahih* – sound narrations–and that al-Bazzar narrated it with a chain whose narrators are the men of sound hadith except for Muhammad ibn Amir al-Antaki, and he is *thiqa* –trustworthy. In the version Tabarani narrated from Ibn Amr in *al-Mujam al kabir* and *al-Mujam al-awsat* the Prophet repeats three times: "When the dissensions take place, belief will be in Syria." One manuscript bears: "Safety will be in Sham." al-Haythami said the men in its chain are those of sound hadith except for Ibn Lahia, and he is fair *(hasan).*

(3) al-Tabarani relates from Abd Allah ibn Hawala that the Prophet said: "I saw on the night that I was enraptured a white column resembling a pearl, which the angels were carrying. I said to them: What are you carrying? They replied: The Column of the Book. We have been ordered to place it in Sham. Later, in my sleep, I saw that the Column of the Book was snatched away from under my headrest *(wisadati).* I began to fear lest Allah the Almighty had abandoned the people of the earth. My eyes followed where it went. It was a brilliant light in front of me. Then I saw it was placed in Sham." Abd Allah ibn Hawala said: "O Messenger of Allah, choose for me (where I should go)." The Prophet said: *alayka bi al-sham* – "You must go to Sham." *Al-hafiz* al-Haythami said in *Majma al-zawaid*: "The narrators in its chain of transmission are all those of sound hadith, except Salih ibn Rustum, and he is trustworthy *(thiqa).*"

(4) Imam Ahmad ibn Hanbal relates in his *Musnad* (1:112): The people of Sham were mentioned in front of Ali ibn Abi Talib while he was in Iraq, and they said to him: Curse them, O Commander of the Believers. He replied: No, I heard the Messenger of Allah say: "The Substitutes *(al-abdal)* are in Sham and they are forty men, every time one of them dies, Allah substitutes another in his place. By means of them Allah brings down the rain, gives (Muslims) victory over their enemies, and averts punishment from the people of Syria." Al-Haythami said in *Majma al-zawaid*: "The men in its chains are all those of sound hadith except for Sharih ibn Ubayd, and he is trustworthy *(thiqa).*" There are more hadiths on the *abdal* which we cite elsewhere in the present work.

you had answered him your Community would have followed Judaism.'

The Prophet (ﷺ) continued traveling and he heard someone calling him from his left, 'O Muhammad, look at me, I want to ask you something!' But the Prophet (ﷺ) did not respond. Then he asked, 'Who was this, O Gabriel?' He replied, 'This is the herald of the Christians. If you had answered him your Community would have followed Christianity.'

The Prophet (ﷺ) continued traveling and then passed by a woman with bare arms, decked with every female ornament Allah had created. She said, 'O Muhammad, look at me, I need to ask you something.' But he did not look at her. Then he asked, 'Who was this, O Gabriel?' He replied, "[She was from among] the worldly, (*al-dunya*). If you had answered her, your Community would have preferred the world to the hereafter.'

As the Prophet (ﷺ) traveled on, he passed by an old man who was a distance away from his path saying, 'Come here O Muhammad!' The Prophet (ﷺ) went on and then asked, 'Who was that, O Gabriel?' Gabriel replied, "That was Allah's enemy, Iblis. He wanted you to incline towards him.'

He went on and passed by an old woman on the roadside who said, 'O Muhammad, look at me, I need to ask you something.' But he did not look at her. Then he asked, 'Who was that, O Gabriel?' Gabriel replied, 'The world has as much left to live as the remaining lifetime of this old woman.'

(Al-Shami added:) As he went on he was met by some of Allah's creatures who said, 'Peace be upon you, O First One! Peace upon you, O Last One! Peace be upon you, O Gatherer!' Gabriel said to him, 'Return their greeting,' and he did. Then he saw them another time and they said the same thing. Then he saw them a third time and again they greeted him. He asked, 'Who are they, O Gabriel?' He replied, 'Abraham, Moses and Jesus (ﷺ).'

The Prophet (ﷺ) then passed by Moses (ﷺ) as he was praying in his grave at a place of red sandhills. He was tall, with long hair and brown complexion, similar to one of the *shanua*–the (Yemeni) men of pure lineage and manly virtue. He was saying with a loud voice, "You have honored him and preferred him!" Then the Prophet (ﷺ) greeted him and he returned his greeting. Moses (ﷺ) asked, "Who is that with you, O Gabriel?" Gabriel replied, "This is Ahmad." Moses (ﷺ) said, "Welcome to the Arabian Prophet (ﷺ) who acted perfectly with his Community!" and he made an invocation for blessing on his behalf. Then he said, "Ask ease for your Community."

They continued traveling and the Prophet (ﷺ) asked, 'O Gabriel, who was that?' Gabriel replied, 'That was Moses son of Imran.' The Prophet (ﷺ) asked, 'Who was he reprimanding?' Gabriel said, 'He was reprimanding his Lord.' The Prophet (ﷺ) asked, 'He reprimands his Lord and raises his voice against his Lord?!' Gabriel said, 'Allah the Exalted is familiar with the bluntness of Moses.'

He passed by a large tree whose fruit seemed like a thornless berry (of the kind that gives shade to men and cattle). Under it an old man was resting with his dependents. There were lamps and a great light could be seen. The Prophet (ﷺ) asked, 'Who is that, O Gabriel?' Gabriel replied, 'Your father Abraham (ﷺ).' The Prophet (ﷺ) greeted him and Abraham (ﷺ) returned his greeting and asked, 'Who is this with you, O Gabriel?' Gabriel replied, 'He is your son Ahmad.' Abraham (ﷺ) said: 'Welcome to the unlettered Arabian Prophet (ﷺ) who has conveyed the message of his Lord and acted with perfect sincerity with his Community! O my son, you are going to meet your Lord tonight, and your Community is the last and the weakest of all Communities– therefore, if you are able to have your need fulfilled concerning your Community, or most of it, be sure to do it!' Then Abraham (ﷺ) invoked for goodness on his behalf.

They continued traveling until they reached the valley that is in the city– that is, the Hallowed House (Jerusalem)–when lo and behold! hell was shown to them like a carpet unfolded. They (the Companions) asked, 'O Messenger of Allah, how was it?' He replied, 'Like cinders."

He continued traveling until he reached the city of the Hallowed House and he entered it by its southern gate. He dismounted the Buraq and tied it at the gate of the mosque, using the ring by which the prophets tied it before him. One narration states that Gabriel went to the Rock and placed his fingers in it, piercing it, then he tied the Buraq using the spot he had hollowed out.

The Prophet (ﷺ) entered the mosque from a gate through which the sun and the moon could be seen when they set. He prayed two cycles of prayer and did not tarry long before a large throng of people had gathered. The Prophet (ﷺ) recognized all the prophets, some standing in prayer, some bowing, some prostrating. Then a caller called out to the prescribed prayer and the final call to prescribed prayer was made. They rose and stood in lines, waiting for the one who would lead them. Gabriel took the hand of the Prophet (ﷺ) and brought him forward. He led them in two cycles of prescribed prayer.[27]

The following is related from Kab: Gabriel raised the call to prescribed prayer. The angels descended from the heaven. Allah gathered all the messengers and prophets. Then the Prophet (ﷺ) prayed as the leader of the angels and messengers. When he left Gabriel asked him, 'O Muhammad, do you know who prayed behind you?' He said no. Gabriel said, 'Every single prophet whom Allah has ever sent."

(Al-Shami adds:) Abu Hurayra's narration related by al-Hakim who declared it sound, and by al-Bayhaqi, states: 'The Prophet (ﷺ) met the spirits of the prophets. They glorified their Lord, after which Abraham (ﷺ) said: "Praise to Allah Who has taken me as His intimate friend, Who has given me an immense kingdom, Who has made me a prayerful Community and one by whom prayer is led, Who has rescued me from the fire and made it cool and safe for me!"'

Then Moses (ﷺ) glorified his Lord and said: 'Praise be to Allah Who has spoken to me directly,

---

27 Shaykh Muhammad ibn Alawi said, "This took place before his ascension according to the highest probability;" Najm al-Din al-Ghiti said, "The narrations agree to the fact that the Prophet prayed among the other Prophets in Jerusalem before his ascension." This is one of the two possibilities mentioned by Qadi Iyad. *Hafiz* Ibn Hajar said, "This is apparently the case. The second possibility is that he prayed among them after he came down from the heaven, and they came down also." Ibn Kathir also declared the former scenario as the sound one. Some said, "What is the objection to the possibility that the Prophet prayed among them twice, since some of the hadiths mention that he led them in prayer after his ascent?"

Who has brought to pass the destruction of Pharaoh and the salvation of the Children of Israel at my hands, and Who has made from among my Community a people who guide others through truth and establish justice upon it!'

Then David (ﷺ) glorified his Lord and said: 'Praise be to Allah Who has brought me an immense kingdom, Who has softened iron for my hands, and subjected to me the mountains and the birds which laud Him, and has given me wisdom and unmistakable judgment in my speech'!

Then Solomon (ﷺ) glorified his Lord and said: 'Praise be to Allah Who has subjected the winds to my command as well as the satans, so that they did as I wished and constructed for me elevated sanctuaries, images, large bowls the size of ponds, and vessels fixed in their spot (due to their size), Who has taught me the language of birds and has brought me a part of every good thing, Who has subjected to me the armies of the satans and the birds and has preferred me over many of His believing servants, Who has brought me an immense kingdom which no one after me may possess, and Who has made my kingdom a goodly one wherein there is no reckoning nor punishment!

Then Jesus (ﷺ) son of Mary glorified his Lord and said: 'Praise be to Allah Who has made me His Word, Who has fashioned me after Adam's likeness whom He created out of earth then said to him, "Be," and he was, Who has taught me the Book and the Wisdom and the Torah and the Gospels, Who has caused me to heal the blind and the leper and to raise the dead by Allah's permission, Who has raised me and cleansed me and granted me and my mother protection against the cursed devil, so that the devil had no path by which to harm us!' (End of al-Shami's addition).

Every prophet then glorified his Lord in the best of language, and the Prophet (ﷺ) said: 'All of you have glorified their Lord and I am going to glorify my Lord also: *al-hamdu lillah al-ladhi arsalani rahmatan li al-alamin wa kaffatan li al-nasi bashiran wa nadhira wa anzala alayya al-qurana fihi tibyanun li kulli shay wa jaala ummati khayra ummatin ukhri-jat li al-nas wa jaala ummati wasatan wa jaala ummati hum al-awwaluna wa al-akhirun wa shara-ha li sadri wa wadaa anni wazri wa rafaa li dhikri wa jaalani falihan khatiman!* (praise belongs to Allah Who has sent me, a mercy to the worlds sent to all without exception, a bearer of glad tidings and a warner, who has caused to descend upon me the Quran in which there is a perfect exposition of all things, who has made my Community the best Community ever brought out for the benefit of mankind, who has made my Community a mean and a middle, who has made my Community in truth the first and the last of all Communities, who has expanded my breast and has relieved me of my burden, who has exalted my name, and has made me the Opener and the Sealer! upon hearing this Abraham said, "In this has Muhammad vested you!)."'

Then they brought up the matter of the Hour and referred it to Abraham (ﷺ), but he said, 'I have no knowledge of it.' They turned to Moses (ﷺ) but he said, 'I have no knowledge of it.' They turned to Jesus (ﷺ) and he said: 'As for the time when it shall befall, no one knows it except Allah. As for what my Lord has assured me (concerning what precedes it), then the Dajjal or Antichrist will come forth and I will face him with two rods. At my sight he shall melt like lead. Allah shall cause his destruction as soon as he sees me. It will be so that the very stones will say, "O Muslim, behind me hides a disbeliever, therefore come and kill him!" And Allah shall cause them all to die.

'People will then return to their countries and nations. At that time Yajuj and Majuj (Gog and Magog) shall come out. They will come from every direction. They will trample all nations underfoot. Whatever they come upon they will destroy. They will drink up every body of water.

'At last the people will come to me complaining about them. At that time I will invoke Allah against them so that He will destroy them and cause their death until the whole earth will reek of their stench.

Allah will send down rain that shall carry their bodies away and hurl them into the sea.

'I have been assured by my Lord that once all this takes place then the Hour will be as the pregnant mother at the last stages of her pregnancy. Her family does not know when she shall suddenly give birth by night or by day.' (End of al-Shami's addition)

The Prophet (☸) then felt the greatest thirst that he had ever felt, whereupon Gabriel brought him a vessel of wine and a vessel of milk. He chose the latter. Gabriel said, 'You have chosen natural disposition (fitra). If you had taken the wine, your Community would have strayed from the right way and none but a few of them would have followed you.'28

Another narration states: There were three vessels and the third contained water. Gabriel said, 'If you had taken the water, your Community would have perished by drowning.'

Another narration states that one of the vessels presented to him contained honey instead of water, and that he then saw the wide-eyed maidens of paradise to the left of the Rock. He greeted them and they returned his greeting. Then he asked them something and they replied with an answer that cools the eyes.

Then the Prophet (☸) was brought the ladder by which the spirits of the children of Adam ascend. Creation never saw a more beautiful object. It had alternate stairs of silver and gold and came down from the highest and amplest garden of paradise, jannat al-firdaws. It was incrusted with pearls and surrounded with angels on its right and left.

The Prophet (☸) began his ascent with Gabriel until they reached one of the gates of the nearest

---

28 The Prophet said, "Every child is born with a natural disposition (kullu mawludin yuladu ala al-fitra); then his parents make him Jewish, Christian or Zoroastrian. It is the same with the animal which delivers a perfect baby animal. Do you find it missing anything?" Bukhari narrates it. Muslim omits the mention of the animal. Tirmidhi's narration (hasan sahih) also omits it, but adds: "O Messenger of Allah, what if the child dies before that?" He replied: "Allah knows best what they would have done." The hadith master al-Zabidi said in his commentary on Ghazali's Ihya entitled Ithaf al-sadat al-muttaqin bi sharh ihya ulum al-din (The gift of the godwary masters: commentary on Ghazali's "Giving life to the sciences of the Religion"): "Born with a natural disposition: the definite case indicates that it is commonly known, and it consists in Allah's disposition with which He endows all people, that is, the innate character with which He creates them and which predisposes them to accept Religion and to differentiate between the wrong and the right." al-Zabidi, Ithaf al-Sadat al-muttaqin (7:233).

heaven called *bab al-hafazha*. There an angel stood
guard, named Ismail, who was the custodian of the
nearest heaven. He inhabits the wind. He never
ascends to the heaven nor descends to earth except on
the day that the Prophet (ﷺ) died, blessings and
peace upon him. In front of him stood seventy thousand angels, each angel commanding an army of seventy thousand more.

Gabriel asked for the gate to be opened. Someone
asked:
– 'Who is this?'
– 'Gabriel.'
– 'Who is with you?'
– 'Muhammad.'
– 'Has he been sent for?'
– 'Yes.'
– 'Welcome to him, from his family! May Allah
grant him long life, a brother (of ours) and a deputy
(of Allah), and what an excellent brother and deputy!
What an excellent visit is this!'

The gate was opened. When they went in they saw
Adam (ﷺ) the father of humanity, as he was on the
day Allah created him in his complete form. The spirits of the prophets and of his believing offspring were
being shown to him, whereupon he would say, "A
goodly spirit and a goodly soul, put it in the highest
(*illiyyin*)!" Then the spirits of his unbelieving offspring would be shown to him and he would say, "A
foul spirit and a foul soul, put it in the lowest layer of
hell (*sijjin*)!"

The Prophet (ﷺ) saw to Adam's right great dark
masses and a gate exuding a fragrant smell, and to
his left great dark masses and a gate exuding a foul,
putrid smell. Whenever Adam (ﷺ) looked to his right
he would smile and be happy, and whenever he looked
to his left he would be sad and weep. The Prophet (ﷺ)
greeted him and Adam (ﷺ) returned his greeting and
said, 'Welcome to the righteous son and the righteous
Prophet (ﷺ)!'

The Prophet (ﷺ) asked, 'Who is that, O Gabriel?'
Gabriel replied: 'He is your father Adam (ﷺ) and the
dark throngs are the souls of his children. Those on
the right are the people of paradise and those on the

left are the people of the fire. Whenever he looks to his right he smiles and is glad, and whenever he looks to his left he is sad and weeps. The door to his right is the gate of paradise. Whenever he sees those of his offspring enter it he smiles happily. The door to his left is the gate of hell. Whenever he sees those of his offspring enter it he weeps sadly.'

(Al-Shami added:) Then the Prophet (ﷺ) continued for a little while. He saw a tablespread in which there were pieces of (good) meat which no one approached, and another tablespread in which were pieces of rotten meat which stank, surrounded by people who were eating it. The Prophet (ﷺ) asked, 'O Gabriel, who are these people?' He replied, 'These are those of your Community who abandon what is lawful and go to what is unlawful.'

(Another version says:) The Prophet (ﷺ) saw a great deal of people gathered around a tablespread in which was set grilled meat of the best kind one had ever seen. Near the table there was some carrion decaying. The people were coming to the carrion to eat from it, and they were leaving the grilled meat untouched. The Prophet (ﷺ) asked, 'Who are they, O Gabriel?' Gabriel replied, "The adulterers (al-zunat); they make lawful what Allah has made unlawful, and they abandon what Allah has made lawful for them."

Then the Prophet (ﷺ) went on for a little while. He saw groups of people who had bellies as large as houses, and there were snakes in them that could be seen through their skins. Every time one of those people stood up he would fall again and he would say, 'O Allah, don't make the Hour of Judgment rise yet!' Then they meet the people of Pharaoh on the road and the latter trample them underfoot. (The Prophet (ﷺ) said,) 'I heard them clamoring to Allah.' He asked, 'O Gabriel, who are these people?' He replied, "They are those of your Community who eat up usury. They cannot stand up except in the manner of those whom satan touches with possession.'

Then the Prophet (ﷺ) went on for a little while. He saw groups of people whose lips resembled the lips of camels. Their mouths were being pried open and they would be stoned. One version says: A rock from hell was placed in their mouths and then it would come out again from their posteriors. (The Prophet (ﷺ) said,) 'I heard them clamoring to Allah.' He asked, 'O Gabriel, who are these people?' Gabriel replied, 'They are those of your Community who eat up the property of orphans and commit injustice. They are eating nothing but a fire for their bellies, and they shall be roasted in it.'

Then the Prophet (ﷺ) went on for a little while. He saw women suspended by their breasts and others hanging upside down, (and the Prophet (ﷺ) said,) 'I heard them clamoring to Allah.' He asked, 'Who are these, O Gabriel?' He replied, 'These are the women who commit fornication and then kill their children.'

Then the Prophet (ﷺ) went on for a little while. He saw groups of people whose sides were being cut off for meat and they were being devoured. They were being told, 'Eat, just as you used to eat the flesh of your brother.' The Prophet (ﷺ) said, 'O Gabriel, who are these?' He replied, 'They are the slanderers of your Community who would bring shame to others.'" (End of al-Shami's addition.)

Then the Prophet (ﷺ) continued for a little while, and he found the consumers of usury and of the property of orphans, and the fornicators and adulterers, and others, in various loathsome states as those that have been described, and worse.

Then they ascended to the second heaven. Gabriel asked for the gate to be opened. Someone asked:

– Who is this?'
– 'Gabriel.'
– 'Who is with you?'
– 'Muhammad.'
– 'Has he been sent for?'
– 'Yes.'
– 'Welcome to him, from his family! May Allah grant him long life, a brother (of ours) and a deputy (of Allah), and what excellent brother and deputy! What an excellent visit is this!'

The gate was opened. When they went in they saw the sons of the two sisters, Jesus (ﷺ) son of Mary and John (ﷺ) son of Zakariyya. They resembled each other in clothing and hair. Each had with him a large company of their people. Jesus (ﷺ) was curly-haired, of medium build, leaning towards fair complexion, with hair let down as if he were coming out of the bath. He resembled Urwa ibn Masud al-Thaqafi.[29]

The Prophet (ﷺ) greeted them and they returned his greeting. Then they said, 'Welcome to the righteous brother and the righteous Prophet (ﷺ)!' Then they invoked for goodness on his behalf.

After this the Prophet (ﷺ) and Gabriel ascended to the third heaven. Gabriel asked for the gate to be opened. Someone said:
– 'Who is it?'
– 'Gabriel.'
– 'Who is with you?'
– 'Muhammad.'
– 'Has he been sent for?'
– 'Yes.'
– 'Welcome to him, from his family! May Allah grant him long life, a brother (of ours) and a deputy (of Allah), and what excellent brother and deputy! What an excellent visit is this!'

The gate was opened. When they came in they saw Joseph (ﷺ), and with him stood a large company of his people. The Prophet (ﷺ) greeted him and he returned his greeting and said, 'Welcome to the righteous brother and the righteous Prophet (ﷺ)!' Then he invoked for goodness on his behalf.

Joseph (ﷺ) had been granted the gift of beauty. (One narration says:) He was the most handsome creation that Allah had ever created and he surpassed people in beauty the way the full moon surpasses all other stars. The Prophet (ﷺ) asked, 'Who is this, O Gabriel?' Gabriel replied, "Your brother Joseph (ﷺ)."

29 Urwa ibn Masud al-Thaqafi was one of the dignitaries of the town of Taif. Ibn Hajar in his *Isaba* relates that he alone responded to the Prophet's invitation to that city by following him and declaring his acceptance of Islam. Then he asked for permission to return to his people and speak to them. The Prophet said: "I fear lest they harm you." He said: "They would not even wake me up if they saw me sleeping." Then he returned. When he began to invite them to Islam, they rejected him. One morning as he stood outside his house making *adhan*, a man shot him with an arrow. As he lay dying he was asked: "What do you think about your death now?" He replied: "It is a gift given me out of Allah's generosity." When news of this reached the Prophet he said: "He is like the man of *Ya Sin* when he came to his people," a reference to 36:20-27. Ibn Hajar also mentions that it is from Urwa that Abu Nuaym narrated (with a weak chain) that the Prophet took the women's pledge of allegiance at Hudaybiyya by touching the water of a pail in which they had dipped their hands.

Then they ascended to the fourth heaven. Gabriel asked for the gate to be opened. Someone asked:
– 'Who is it?'
– 'Gabriel.'
– 'Who is with you?'
– 'Muhammad.'
– 'Has he been sent for?'
– 'Yes.'
– 'Welcome to him, from his family! May Allah grant him long life, a brother (of ours) and a deputy (of Allah), and what excellent brother and deputy! What an excellent visit is this!'

The gate was opened. When they went in they saw Idris (🕮). Allah exalted him to a lofty place. The Prophet (🕮) greeted him and he returned his greeting and said, 'Welcome to the righteous brother and the righteous Prophet (🕮)!' Then he invoked for goodness on his behalf.

Then they ascended to the fifth heaven. Gabriel asked for the gate to be opened. Someone asked:
– 'Who is it?'
– 'Gabriel.'
– 'Who is with you?'
– 'Muhammad.'
– 'Has he been sent for?'
– 'Yes.'
– 'Welcome to him, from his family! May Allah grant him long life, a brother (of ours) and a deputy (of Allah), and what excellent brother and deputy! What an excellent visit is this!'

The gate was opened. When they went in they saw Aaron. Half of his beard was white and the other half was black. It almost reached his navel due to its length. Surrounding him were a company of the children of Israel listening to him as he was telling them a story. The Prophet (🕮) greeted him and he returned his greeting and said, 'Welcome to the righteous brother and the righteous Prophet (🕮)!' Then he invoked for goodness on his behalf. The Prophet (🕮) asked, 'Who is he, O Gabriel?' Gabriel replied, 'He is the man who is beloved among his people, Aaron son of Imran."

Then they ascended to the sixth heaven. Gabriel

asked for the gate to be opened. Someone asked:
– 'Who is it?'
– 'Gabriel.'
– 'Who is with you?'
– 'Muhammad.'
– 'Has he been sent for?'
– 'Yes.'
– 'Welcome to him, from his family! May Allah grant him long life, a brother (of ours) and a deputy (of Allah), and what excellent brother and deputy! What an excellent visit is this!'

The gate was opened. The Prophet (ﷺ) passed by prophets who had with them less than ten followers in all, while others had a large company, and others had not even one follower.

Then he saw a huge dark mass (*sawad azim*) that covered the firmament. He asked, 'What is this throng?' He was told, "This is Moses (ﷺ) and his people. Now raise your head and look.' He raised his head and saw another huge dark mass that was covering the firmament from every direction he looked. He was told, 'This is your Community, and besides these there are seventy thousand of them that will enter paradise without giving account.'

As they went in the Prophet (ﷺ) saw Moses (ﷺ) son of Imran (again), a tall man with brown complexion, similar to one of the *shanua*– the (Yemeni) men of pure lineage and manly virtue–with abundant hair. If he had two shirts on him, still his hair would exceed them. The Prophet (ﷺ) greeted him and he returned his greeting and said, 'Welcome to the righteous brother and the righteous Prophet (ﷺ)!' Then he invoked for goodness on his behalf and said, 'The people claim that among the sons of Adam I am more honored by Allah than this one, but it is he who is more honored by Allah than me!"

When the Prophet (ﷺ) reached him Moses (ﷺ) wept. He was asked, "What is it that makes you weep?" He replied, "I weep because a child that was sent after me will cause more people to enter paradise from his Community than will enter from mine. The children of Israel claim that among the children of Adam I am the one most honored by Allah, but here is one man among the children of Adam who has come after me in the world while I am in the next world (and is more honored). If he were only by himself I would not mind, but he has his Community with him!"

Then they ascended to the seventh heaven. Gabriel asked for the gate to be opened. Someone asked:

- 'Who is it?'
- 'Gabriel.'
- 'Who is with you?'
- 'Muhammad."
- 'Has he been sent for?'
- 'Yes.'
- 'Welcome to him, from his family! May Allah grant him long life, a brother (of ours) and a deputy (of Allah), and what excellent brother and deputy! What an excellent visit is this!'

The gate was opened. The Prophet (ﷺ) saw Abraham (ﷺ) the Friend sitting at the gate of paradise on a throne of gold the back of which was leaning against the Inhabited House (al-bayt al-mamur). With him was a company of his people. The Prophet (ﷺ) greeted him and he returned his greeting and said, 'Welcome to the righteous son and the righteous Prophet (ﷺ)!"[30]

Then Abraham (ﷺ) said, 'Order your Community to increase their seedlings of Paradise for its soil is excellent and its land is plentiful.' The Prophet (ﷺ) said, 'What are the seedlings of paradise?' He replied, 'La hawla wa la quwwata illa billah al-ali al-azhim (there is no change nor might except with Allah the High, the Almighty).'

(Another version says:) 'Convey my greetings to your Community and tell them that Paradise has excellent soil and sweet water, and that its seedlings are: subhan Allah Glory to Allah wa al-hamdu lillah and Praise to Allah wa la ilaha ill Allah and there is no god but Allah wallahu akbar and Allah is greater.

With Abraham (ﷺ) were sitting a company of people with pristine faces similar to the whiteness of a blank page, and next to them were people with something in their faces. The latter stood and entered

---

30 Shaykh Muhammad ibn Alawi said: "Mamur means inhabited with the remembrance of Allah and the great number of angels."

a river in which they bathed. Then they came out having purified some of their hue. Then they entered another river and bathed and came out having purified some more. Then they entered a third river and bathed and purified themselves and their hue became like that of their companions. They came back and sat next to them.

The Prophet (攀) said, 'O Gabriel, who are those with white faces and those who had something in their hues, and what are these rivers in which they entered and bathed?' He replied, 'The ones with white faces are a people who never tarnished their belief with injustice or disobedience; those with something in their hues are a people who would mix good deeds with bad ones, then they repented and Allah relented towards them. As for these rivers, the first is Allah's mercy (*rahmat Allah*), the second his favor (*nimat Allah*), and the third and their Lord gave them a pure beverage to drink (*wa saqahum rabbuhum sharaban tahuran*) (76:21).'"

Then the Prophet (攀) was told, 'This is your place and the place of your Community.' He saw that his Community were divided into two halves: one half were wearing clothes that seemed as white as a blank page, the other were wearing clothes that seemed the color of ashes or dust. He entered the Inhabited House and those who were wearing the white clothes entered with him. Those that wore ash-colored clothes were no longer able to see him, and yet they were in the best of states. The Prophet (攀) prayed in the Inhabited House together with those of the believers that were with him.

Every day seventy thousand angels enter the Inhabited House, who shall never return to it until the Day of Resurrection. The angels who have entered it never see it again. This House is exactly superimposed over the Kabah. If one stone fell from it, it would fall on top of the Kabah.

One version states that the presentation of the three vessels, the Prophet's choice of the vessel of milk, and Gabriel's approval took place at this point.

(Al-Shami adds:) Al-Tabarani cites this hadith with a sound chain, 'The night I was enraptured I passed by the heavenly host, and lo and behold!

Gabriel was like the worn-out saddle-cloth on the camel's back from fear of his Lord." One of al-Bazzar's narrations states, "like a saddle-blanket that clings to the ground.'[31]

Then the Prophet (صلى الله عليه وسلم) was raised up to the Lote-tree of the Farthest Limit. There ends whatever ascends from the earth before it is seized, and whatever descends from above before it is seized.[32]

It is a tree from the base of which issue rivers whose water is never brackish (it does not change in taste, or color, or smell, and the sweat of those who drink it in paradise has the fragrance of musk), and rivers of milk whose taste does not change after it is drunk, and rivers of wine which brings only pleasure to those who drink it, and rivers of purified honey. Someone on his mount could travel under its shade for seventy years and still not come out of it. The lotus fruit that grows on it resembles the jars of Hijar (near Madina). Its leaves are shaped like the ears of the she-elephant, and each leaf could wrap up this Community entirely. One version says, one of its leaves could wrap up all creatures.

On top of each leaf there was an angel who covered it with colors that cannot be described. Whenever he covered it by Allah's order it would change. One version says: It would turn into sapphire and chrysolite the beauty of which it is impossible for

31 Shaykh Muhammad ibn Alawi said: "Of the same meaning is the hadith: *kun hilsan min ahlasi baytik* Be one of the saddle blankets of your horse, that is: keep to it in times of dissension.

32 Al-Dardir said, "This is the eighth ascension, meaning that it is the ascension to what is higher than the Lote-tree by means of the eighth step, so that the Prophet reached the top height of its branches in the eighth firmament which is called *al-Kursi* –the Chair, or Footstool–which is made of a white pearl. This is found in al-Qalyubi, and it is the apparent sense of the account. However, it is contradicted by what is mentioned later: "Then he came to the *Kawthar*," because the *Kawthar*, like the remainder of the rivers, flows from the base of the Tree, not from its top, and the account goes on to say after this: "Then he was raised up to the Lote-tree of the Farthest Limit." It follows that the raising up to the Lote-tree took place more than once, but undoubtedly this is dubious for whoever ponders it. I saw in al-Ajhuri's account at this point: "Then he **came** to the Lote-tree of the farthest boundary, there ends etc." and this is correct as it does not signify being raised up. This makes it clear that he came to the Tree and saw at its base the rivers – which are soon to be mentioned – and he travelled towards the *Kawthar*. What the narrator said later: "Then he was raised to the Lote-tree of the Farthest Limit etc." indicates that the eighth ascension took place at that later point and that the present stage is only an exposition of his coming to the **base** of the Tree which is in the seventh heaven. Another narration states that it is in the sixth heaven. What harmonizes the two is that its base is in the sixth heaven while its branches and trunk are in the seventh."

anyone to praise according to its merit. On it were moths of gold.

From the base of the tree issued four (more) rivers: two hidden rivers and two visible ones. The Prophet (ﷺ) asked, 'What are these, O Gabriel? He replied, "As for the hidden ones, they are two rivers of Paradise. The visible ones are the Nile and the Euphrates."'[33]

(Al-Shami added that one version says): At the base of the tree ran a source called Salsabil. From it issued two rivers; one is the Kawthar. (The Prophet (ﷺ) said,) 'I saw it flowing impetuously, roaring, at the speed of arrows. Near it were pavilions of pearl (*lulu*), sapphire (*yaqut*), and chrysolite (*zabarjad*) on top of which nested green birds more delicate than any you have ever seen. On its banks were vessels of gold and silver. It ran over pebbles made of sapphire and emerald (*zumurrud*). Its water was whiter than milk.'

The Prophet (ﷺ) took one of the vessels and scooped some water and drank. It was sweeter than honey and more fragrant than musk. Gabriel said to him, 'This is the river that Allah has given you as a special gift, and the other river is the River of Mercy.' The Prophet (ﷺ) bathed in it and his past and future sins were forgiven. (End of al-Shami's addition.)

(One version says:) At the Lote-tree of the Farthest Limit the Prophet (ﷺ) saw Gabriel (in his angelic form). He had six hundred wings. Every single wing could cover the entire firmament. From his wings embellishments were strewn in all directions, such as rare pearls and sapphires of a kind Allah alone knows. Then the Prophet (ﷺ) was taken to the Kawthar and entered Paradise. Lo and behold! It contains what no eye has seen, nor ear heard, nor human mind ever imagined. On its gate he saw written: *al-sadaqatu bi ashrin amthaliha wa al-qardu bi*

---

33 Ibn Kathir said, "What is meant by this, and Allah knows best, is that these two rivers (the Nile and the Euphrates) resemble the rivers of Paradise in their purity and sweetness and fluidity and such of their qualities, as the Prophet said in the hadith narrated by Abu Hurayra: *al-ajwa min al-janna* "Date pastry is from paradise," that is: it resembles the fruit of Paradise, not that it itself originates in Paradise. If that were the meaning then the senses would testify to the contrary. Therefore the meaning which imposes itself is other than that. Similarly the source of origin of these rivers is on earth."

thamaniyati ashara (charity is repaid tenfold, and a goodly loan eighteenfold).

The Prophet (ﷺ) asked, 'O Gabriel, how can the loan be more meritorious than charity?' Gabriel replied, 'Because one asking for charity may still have some need left, while when a borrower borrows, his need is fulfilled.'

The Prophet (ﷺ) continued to travel until he reached rivers of milk whose taste does not change, and rivers of wine which bring only pleasure to those who drink it, and rivers of honey purified, and over-hanging those rivers were domes of hollowed pearl whose circumference is as wide as the Aquarius star.

(Another narration says:) Above the rivers were pommels resembling the hides of the humped camels. Its birds were like the Bactrian camel. Upon hearing this Abu Bakr said, 'O Messenger of Allah, they are certainly delicate!' The Prophet (ﷺ) replied, 'And daintier to eat yet, and certainly I hope that you shall eat from them.'[34]

The Prophet (ﷺ) then saw the Kawthar and on its banks were domes of hollowed pearl. The soil of its banks was extremely fragrant musk. Then the Fire was shown to him. In it he saw Allah's wrath and His punishment and sanction. Were rocks and iron to be thrown into it the fire would consume them complete-ly. In it were a people who were eating carrion. The Prophet (ﷺ) said, 'Who are these people, O Gabriel?' Gabriel replied, 'They are those who ate the flesh of people.' Then the Prophet (ﷺ) saw Malik, the custo-dian of the fire. He was a grim figure whose face expressed anger. The Prophet (ﷺ) greeted him first. Then the gates of the fire were closed as he stood out-side, and he was raised up beyond the Lote-tree of the Farthest Limit, and a cloud concealed him from everything else, and Gabriel stayed back.[35]

---

34 This is an indication of the rank of Abu Bakr in Paradise, as the Prophet's hope, like his petition, is granted. Shaykh Muhammad ibn Alawi also said: "From all this it can be known that paradise and the Fire exist already, and that the Lote-tree of the Farthest Boundary is outside paradise.

35 Shaykh Muhammad ibn Alawi said the Prophet's greeting of Malik before Malik greeted him first agrees with the subsequent wording of more than one narrator whereby the Prophet said, 'I greeted him and he returned my greeting and welcomed me, but he did not smile at me' etc. and this is found in some of the narrations. However, the correct narration, as the compiler and others have said, is that it is Malik who greeted the Prophet first in order to dispel the harshness of his sight since his face showed severity and anger. It is possible to harmonize the two versions with the fact

The Prophet (ﷺ) was taken up to a point where he heard the scratching of the Pens (writing the divine decree). He saw a man who had disappeared into the light of the Throne. He asked, 'Who was that? Is this an angel?' It was said to him, no. He asked, 'Is he a Prophet (ﷺ)?' Again the answer was no. He asked, 'Who is it then?' The answer was, 'This is a man whose tongue was moist with Allah's remembrance in the world, his heart was attached to the mosques, and he never incurred the curse of his father and mother.'

Then the Prophet (ﷺ) saw his Lord, the Glorious, the Exalted, and he fell prostrate. At that time his Lord spoke to him and said, 'O Muhammad!' He replied, 'At your service, O Lord!' Allah said, 'Ask (sal)!' The Prophet (ﷺ) said: 'You have taken to Yourself Abraham (ﷺ) as a friend. You have given him an immense kingdom. You have spoken to Moses (ﷺ) directly, and have given David (ﷺ) an immense kingdom and softened iron and subjected the mountains to him. You have given Solomon (ﷺ) an immense kingdom, and subjected the *jinn* and men and satans to him, as well as the winds. You have given him a kingdom the like no one may have after him. You have taught Jesus (ﷺ) the Torah and the Gospel, and made him heal those born blind and the lepers, and raise up the dead with Your permission, and You have protected him and his mother from the cursed devil so that the devil had no path by which to harm them!

Allah said, 'And I have taken you to Myself as My beloved.' The narrator said, 'It is written in the Torah: *habibullah* (Allah's Beloved).' Allah continued: 'And I have sent you for all people without exception, a bearer of glad tidings and a warner; and I have expanded your breast for you and relieved you of your burden and exalted your name; and I am not mentioned except you are mentioned with Me; and I have made your Community the best Community ever brought out for the benefit of mankind; and I have

that the Prophet saw Malik more than once, so that Malik was first to greet the Prophet the first time, as we said, while the Prophet was first to greet Malik the second time, in order to dispel estrangement and to inspire familiarity. Know also that the Prophet's sight of Malik was not in the same form that those who are being punished see him.

made your Community a mean and a middle; and I
have made your Community in truth the first and the
last of all Communities; and I have made public
address (al-khutba) impermissible for your
Community unless they first witness that you are My
servant and messenger; and I have placed certain people in your Community with Gospels for hearts (i.e.
repositories of Allah's Book); and I have made you the
first Prophet (ﷺ) created and the last one sent and
the first one heard in My court; and I have given you
Seven of the Oft-Repeated which I gave to no other
Prophet (ﷺ) before you (i.e. Surah al-Fatiha); and I
have given you the last verses of Surah al-Baqara
which constitute a treasure from under My Throne
which I gave to no other Prophet (ﷺ) before you; and
I have given you the Kawthar; and I have given you
eight arrows (i.e. shares in good fortune): Islam, emi-
gration (hijra), jihad, charity (sadaqa), fasting
Ramadan, ordering good, and forbidding evil; and the
day I created the heavens and the earth I made obligatory upon you and upon your Community fifty
prayers. Therefore establish them, you and your
Community."

(Al-Shami added:) Abu Hurayra said: Allah's
Messenger said: My Lord has preferred me over
everyone else (faddalani rabbi); He has sent me as a
mercy to the worlds and to all people without exception, a bearer of glad tidings and a warner; He has
thrown terror into the hearts of my enemies at a distance of a month's travel; he has made spoils of war
lawful for me while they were not lawful for anyone
before me; the entire earth has been made a ritually
pure place of prostration for me; I was given the
words that open, those that close, and those that are
comprehensive in meaning (i.e. I was given the apex
of eloquence); my Community was shown to me and
there is none of the followers and the followed but he
is known to me; I saw that they would come to a people that wear hair-covered sandals; I saw that they
would come to a people of large faces and small eyes
as if they had been pierced with a needle; nothing of
what they would face in the future has been kept hid-

den from me; and I have been ordered to perform fifty prayers daily.

And he has been given three particular merits: He is the Master of Messengers (*sayyid al-mursalin*), the Leader of the Godwary (*imam al-muttaqin*), and the Chief of Those with Signs of Light on Their Faces and Limbs (*qaid al-ghurr al-muhajjalin*). (End of al-Shami's addition.)

One narration says: The Prophet (ﷺ) was given the five daily prescribed prayers and the last verses of *Surah al-Baqara*, and (for his sake) whoever of his Community does not associate anything with Allah is forgiven even the sins that destroy.

Then the cloud that cloaked him was dispelled and Gabriel took him by the hand and sped away with him until he reached Abraham (ﷺ), who did not say anything. Then the Prophet (ﷺ) reached Moses (ﷺ) who asked, 'What did you do, O Muhammad? What obligations did your Lord impose on you and your Community?' He replied, 'He imposed fifty prescribed prayers every day and night on me and my Community.'

Moses (ﷺ) said: 'Return to your Lord and ask Him to lighten your burden and that of your Community for in truth your Community will not be able to carry it. Verily I myself have experienced people's natures before you. I tested the children of Israel and took the greatest pains to hold them to something easier than this, but they were too weak to carry it and they abandoned it. Those of your Community are even weaker in their bodies and constitutions, in their hearts, in their sight, and in their hearing.'

The Prophet (ﷺ) turned to Gabriel to consult him. The latter indicated to him that yes, if he wished, then return. The Prophet (ﷺ) sped back until he reached the Tree and the cloud cloaked him and he fell prostrate. Then he said, 'Lord, make lighter the burden of my Community for verily they are the weakest of all Communities.' He replied, 'I have removed five prayers from their obligation.'

Then the cloud was dispelled and the Prophet (ﷺ) returned to Moses (ﷺ) and told him, 'He has removed five prescribed prayers from my obligation.' He replied, 'Go back to your Lord and ask him to make it less, for in truth your Community will not be able to carry that.' The Prophet (ﷺ) did not cease to go back and forth between Moses (ﷺ) and his Lord, while Allah each time reduced it by five prescribed prayers, until Allah said, 'O Muhammad!' The Prophet (ﷺ) said, 'At Your service, O Lord!' He said: 'Let them be five prescribed prayers every day and night, and let every prayer count as ten. That makes fifty prayers. This word of Mine shall not be changed nor shall My Book be abrogated. Let whoever is about to perform a good deed, even if he does not ultimately do it, receive the reward of doing it, while if he does it, he shall receive it tenfold. Let whoever is about to commit a bad deed, and he does not ultimately do it, let not anything be written against him, while if he does it, let one misdeed be written against him.'

Then the cloud was dispelled and the Prophet (ﷺ) returned to Moses (ﷺ) and told him, 'He has removed five prayers from my obligation.' He replied, 'Go back to your Lord and ask him to make it less, for in truth your Community will not be able to carry that.' The Prophet (ﷺ) said, 'I have gone back again to my Lord until I feel shy from Him. Rather, I accept and submit.' At this a herald called out, 'I have decreed My obligation and have reduced the burden of My servants." Moses (ﷺ) then said to the Prophet (ﷺ), 'Go down in the name of Allah.'

The Prophet (ﷺ) did not pass a throng of angels except they said to him, 'You must practice cupping (alayka bi al-hijama),' and in another version, 'Order cupping to your Community."36

As the Prophet (ﷺ) was descending he asked Gabriel, 'Why did I not see any of the people of heaven except they welcomed me and smiled at me except one. I greeted him and he greeted me back and welcomed me, but he did not smile at me?' He replied. 'That was Malik the custodian of the fire. He never smiled once since the day he was created. If he had ever smiled for anyone, it would have been you.'

When the Prophet (ﷺ) reached the nearest heaven he looked below it and he saw a dense cloud of

36 "Cupping" is defined as the process of drawing blood from the body by scarification (scratches or superficial incisions in the skin) and the application of a cupping glass (in which a partial vacuum is created, as by heat) without scarification, as for relieving internal congestion.

smoke filled with clamor. He asked, 'What is this, O Gabriel?' Gabriel replied, 'These are the devils that swarm over the eyes of human beings so that they will not think about the dominions of the heavens and the earth, or else they would have seen wonders.'

Then he mounted the Buraq again (which he had tied in Jerusalem) and departed. He passed by a caravan of the Quraysh in such-and-such a place (the narrator forgot the name) and saw a camel upon which were tied two containers, a black one and a white one. When he came face to face with the caravan there was a stampede in which the caravan turned around and that camel was thrown down to the ground and its freight broke.

Then the Prophet (ﷺ) passed by another caravan that had lost one of its camels that the tribe of So-and-so had rounded up. The Prophet (ﷺ) greeted them and one of them said, 'This is the voice of Muhammad!' after which the Prophet (ﷺ) returned to his Companions in Makka shortly before morning.

When morning came, he remained alone and, knowing that people would belie him, sat despondently. The enemy of Allah, Abu Jahl, was passing by and he approached and sat down next to him, saying by way of mockery, 'Has anything happened?' The Prophet (ﷺ) replied, 'Yes.' Abu Jahl said, 'And what is that?' The Prophet (ﷺ) replied, 'I was enraptured last night.' Abu Jahl said, 'To where?' The Prophet (ﷺ) replied, 'To the Hallowed House.' Abu Jahl said, 'Then you woke up here among us?' He replied, 'Yes.'

Abu Jahl decided not to belie the Prophet (ﷺ) for fear the Prophet (ﷺ) would deny having said this to him if he went and told the people of Makka, so he said, 'What do you think if I called your people here? Will you tell them what you just told me?' The Prophet (ﷺ) said yes. Abu Jahl cried out, 'O assembly of the Children of Kab ibn Luay, come here!' People left their gatherings and went until they all sat next around the two of them. Abu Jahl said, 'Tell your people what you just told me.' Allah's Messenger (ﷺ) said, 'I was enraptured last night.' They said, 'To where?' The Prophet (ﷺ) replied, 'To the Hallowed House.' They said, 'Then you woke up here among us?' He replied,

'Yes.' There was no one left except he clapped his hands, or held his head in amazement, or clamored and considered it an enormity.

Al-Mutim ibn Adi (who died a disbeliever) said: 'All of your affair before today was bearable, until what you said today. I bear witness that you are a liar (*ana ashhadu annaka kadhibun*). We strike the flanks of the she-camels for one month to reach the Hallowed House, then for another month to come back, and you claim that you went there in one night! By al-Lat, by al-Uzza! I do not believe you.'

Abu Bakr said, 'O Mutim, what an evil thing you said to the son of your brother when you faced him thus and declared him a liar! As for me I bear witness that he spoke the truth (*ana ashhadu annahu sadiqun*).'

The people said, 'O Muhammad, describe the Hallowed House for us. How is it built, what does it look like, how near is it to the mountain?' There were some among them who had traveled there. He began to describe it for them, 'Its structure is like this; its appearance like this; its proximity to the mountain is such-and-such," and he did not stop describing it to them until he began to have doubts about the description. He was seized with an anxiety he had not felt before, whereupon he was immediately brought to the mosque itself (in Jerusalem) and saw it in front of him. He was placed outside the gate of Aqil or Iqal. The people said, 'How many gates does the mosque have?' He had not counted them before. He looked at the gates and began to count them one by one and to inform them. All the while Abu Bakr was saying, 'You have spoken the truth. You have spoken the truth. I bear witness that you are the Messenger of Allah (*sadaqta sadaqta ashhadu annaka rasulullah*).'

The people said, 'As for the description, then, by Allah, he is correct.' They turned to Abu Bakr and said, 'But do you believe what he said, that he went last night to the Hallowed House and came back before morning?' He replied: 'Yes, and I do believe him regarding what is farther than that. I believe the news of heaven he brings, whether in the space of a morning or in that of an evening journey *(naam inni*

*la usaddiquhu fima huwa abadu min dhalika usad-
diqu bi khabari al-samai fi ghudwatin aw rawhatin).'*
    Because of this Abu Bakr was named al-Siddiq,
the Very Truthful, the One Who Never Lies.

    Then they said, 'O Muhammad, tell us about our
caravans.' He replied, 'I saw the caravan of the tribe
of so-and-so as I was coming back. They had lost one
of their camels and were searching for it everywhere.
I reached their mounts and there was no one with
them. I found a water bottle and I drank from it.'[37]

    (The Prophet (ﷺ) continued:) 'Then I reached the
caravan of the tribe of so-and-so in such-and-such a
place. I saw a red camel carrying one black container
and one white one. When I came face to face with the
caravan there was a stampede and that camel fell and
its freight broke. Then I reached the caravan (not pre-
viously mentioned) of the tribe of so-and-so in al-
Tanim. It was headed by a grayish camel on which
was a black hair-cloth and two blackish containers
and here are the (three) caravans about to reach you
from the mountain pass.' They said, 'When will they
arrive?' He replied, 'On the fourth day of the week.' On
that day the Quraysh came out, expecting the caravans. The day passed and they did not arrive. The
Prophet (ﷺ) made an invocation and the day was
extended one more hour during which the sun stood
still, and the caravans came.

    They went to meet the riders and asked them,
"Did you lose a camel?" They said yes. They asked the
second caravan, "Did one red camel of yours shatter
her freight?" They said yes. They asked (the first caravan), "Did anyone lose a water bottle?" One man
said, "I did, by Allah, I had prepared it but none of us
drank it nor was it spilled on the ground!" At this they
accused the Prophet (ﷺ) of sorcery and they said, "Al-
Walid spoke the truth." And Allah revealed the verse:
wa ma jaalna al-ruya al-lati araynaka illa fitnatan li

---

37 Shaykh Muhammad ibn Alawi said, "Doubt has been raised about this report
on the basis of the question how could he allow himself to drink the water without permission from its owner? The answer is that he acted according to the custom of the
Arabs whereby they never refuse milk to whomever passes by and takes it, *a fortiori*
water, and they used to instruct the herdsmen not to prevent wayfarers from taking
milk from the herd (i.e. without asking the owner), and this applies even more to water.
Furthermore, the Prophet comes before the Believers' own selves and properties, and
this applies even more to the disbelievers."

al-nas (*We appointed not the vision which We showed you but as a test for mankind*). (17:60)[38]

The account is finished with praise to Allah and by His grace. May Allah send blessings and utmost, abundant greetings upon our Master Muhammad and his Family and Companions, and praise belongs to Allah the Lord of the worlds!

4.5. THE NIGHT OF MID-SHABAN (*LAYLAT AL-BARAA*) AND THE FIRST NIGHT AND NIGHT OF THE FIRST FRIDAY OF RAJAB (*LAYLAT AL-RAGHAIB*)

Allah said:

inna anzalnahu fi laylatin mubarakatin inna kunna mundhirin
(lo! We revealed it on a blessed night – Lo! We are ever warning)

---

38 Ibn Hisham narrates, "When the fair was due, a number of the Quraysh came to al-Walid ibn al-Mughira, who was a man of some standing, and he addressed them in those words, 'The time of the fair has come round again and representatives of the Arabs will come to you and they will have heard about this fellow of yours, so agree upon one opinion without dispute so that none will give the lie to the other.' They replied, 'You give us your opinion about him.' He said, 'No, you speak and I will listen.' They said, 'He is a *kahin* (seer or giver of oracles).' He said, 'By Allah, he is not that, for he has not the unintelligent murmuring and rhymed speech of the *kahin*.' 'Then he is possessed,' they said. 'No, he is not that,' he said, 'we have seen possessed ones, and here is no choking, spasmodic movements and whispering.' 'Then he is a poet,' they said. 'No, he is no poet, for we know poetry in all its forms and meters.' 'Then he is a sorcerer.' 'No, we have seen sorcerers and their sorcery, and here is no blowing and no knots.' 'Then what are we to say, O Abu Abd al-Shams?' they asked. He replied, 'By Allah, his speech is sweet, his root is a palm-tree whose branches are fruitful, and everything you have said would be known to be false. The nearest thing to the truth is your saying that he is a sorcerer, who has brought a message by which he separates a man from his father, or from his brother, or from his wife, or from his family.'

"At this point they left him, and began to sit on the paths which men take when they come to the fair. They warned everyone who passed them about the Prophet's doings. Allah revealed concerning al-Walid: Leave Me to deal with him whom I created lonely, and then bestowed upon him ample means, and sons abiding in his presence and made life smooth for him. Yet he desires that I should give more. Nay, for lo! He has been stubborn to Our revelations. On him I shall impose a fearful doom. For lo! He did consider; then he planned –Self-destroyed is he, how he planned! Again, self-destroyed is he, how he planned! Then looked he. Then frowned he and showed displeasure. Then turned he away in pride and said: *This is naught else than magic from of old; this is naught else than speech of mortal man. Him shall I fling unto the burning* (74:11-26)."

fiha yufraqu kullu amrin hakim (whereupon
every wise command is made clear)
 amran min indina inna kunna mursilin (as a
command from Our presence–Lo! We are ever sending–)
 *rahmatan min rabbika innahu huwa al-samiu al-
alim* (a mercy from thy Lord. Lo! He is the Hearer, the
Knower). (44:3-6)

The majority of the commentators consider the "blessed
night" in the above verses to refer to the Night of Decree (*laylat al-qadr*), which is considered to be in the month of
Ramadan. However, the commentaries also mention that this
"blessed night" may be that of mid-Shaban (*laylat al-baraa*).
This view is based on the profusion of hadiths on the great merits of the latter. Consequently, the Sharia has commended
observance of that night. Concerning supererogatory worship
on the night of mid-Shaban Suyuti says:

> As for the night of mid-Shaban, it has great merit
> and it is desirable (*mustahabb*) to spend part of it in
> supererogatory worship.[39]

Even Ibn Taymiyya, the putative authority of "Salafis," considered the night of mid-Shaban "a night of superior merit:"

> [Some] said: There is no difference between this
> night (mid-Shaban) and other nights of the year.
> However, the opinion of many of the people of learn-
> ing, and that of the majority of our companions (i.e.
> the Hanbali school) and other than them is that it is
> a night of superior merit, and this is what is indicat-
> ed by the words of Ahmad (ibn Hanbal), in view of the
> many ahadith which are transmitted concerning it,
> and in view of what confirms this from the words and
> deeds transmitted from the early generations (*al-
> athar al-salafiyya*). Some of its merits have been nar-
> rated in the books of hadith of the *musnad* and *sunan*
> types. This holds true even if other things have been
> forged concerning it.[40]

39 Suyuti, *Haqiqat al-sunna wa al-bida aw al-amr bi al-ittiba wa al-nahi an al-ibtida* (1405/1985 ed.) p. 58. He adds: "However, this must be done alone, not in con-gregation."
40 Ibn Taymiyya, *Iqtida al-sirat al-mustaqim* (1369/1950 ed.) p. 302.

Among the hadiths stressing the status of *laylat al-baraa* are the following:

1 Ibn Hibban narrated the following narration from Muadh ibn Jabal:

> The Prophet (ﷺ) said, "*Yattaliu Allahu ila khalqi-hi fi laylati al-nisfi min shabana fayaghfiru li-jamii khalqihi illa li mushrikin aw mushahin* (Allah looks at His creation in the night of mid-Shaban and He for-gives all His creation except for an idolater or a one bent on hatred (*mushahin*).[41]

2 Tirmidhi and Ahmad narrate from Abd Allah ibn Amr:

> Allah looks upon His creatures on the night of mid-Shaban and He forgives all His servants except two: he who is intent on hatred, and he who is intent on murder.[42]

3 Bayhaqi relates from Aisha:

> From Aisha: She said: The Prophet (ﷺ) stood up in prayer during part of the night and made his pros-tration so lengthy that I thought his soul had been taken back. When I saw this I got up and went to move his big toe, whereupon he moved, so I drew back. When he raised his head from prostration and finished praying, he said, 'O Aisha, O fair little one (*humayra*)! Did you think that the Prophet (ﷺ) had broken his agreement with you?' She replied, 'No, by Allah, O Messenger of Allah, but I thought that your soul had been taken back because your stayed in pros-tration for so long.' He said, 'Do you know what night this is?' She said, 'Allah and His Prophet (ﷺ) know best.' He said, 'This is the night of mid-Shaban! Verily Allah the Glorious and Majestic looks at His servants on the night of mid-Shaban, and He forgives those who ask forgiveness, and He bestows mercy on those

41 Ibn Hibban, *Sahih*, ed. Shuayb Arnaut 12:481 #5665. Confirmed sound by the hadith scholar and editor of the *Sahih* Shuayb Arnaut. Haythami said that Tabarani also narrated it in his *Kabir* and *Awsat* with chains containing only trustworthy nar-rators, that is: sound *(sahih)* chains; Ibn Khuzayma included it in his *Sahih*, which has the same level of acceptance among the experts as *Sahih Muslim*; and even Albani included it in his *Silsila sahiha*!

42 Also: Al-Bazzar with a chain he graded as fair *(hasan)* through the great *Tabii* jurist al-Qasim ibn Muhammad ibn Abi Bakr al-Siddiq.

who ask mercy, and He gives a delay to the people of envy and spite in their state.'

Al-Azhari said:

Concerning his words, "broken his agreement with you," this is said to a person who betrays his companion and therefore has not given him his due right.

Bayhaqi continues:

I say: This hadith is missing the Companion in its chain, and is a good hadith (*hadha mursal jayyid*). It is probable that al-Ala ibn al-Harith took it from Makhul, and Allah knows best.[43]

4 Tirmidhi, Ahmad, and Ibn Majah relate:

From Aisha: I missed the Prophet (ﷺ) one night so I went out to al-Baqi (and found him). He said, "Were you afraid that Allah would wrong you and that His Prophet (ﷺ) would wrong you?" I said, "O Messenger of Allah, I thought that you might have gone to visit one of your wives." He said, "Allah Glorious and Exalted descends to the nearest heaven on the night of mid-Shaban and He forgives to more people than the number of hairs on the hides of the sheep of the tribes of Kalb."[44]

Ahmad and Ibn Majah relate:

From Ali ibn Abi Talib: The Prophet (ﷺ) said, "The night of mid-Shaban let all of you spend in prayer (i.e. partly) and its day (i.e. preceding it) in fasting, for Allah descends to the nearest heaven during that night beginning with sunset and says, 'Is there no one asking forgiveness that I may forgive them? Is there no one asking sustenance that I may grant them sustenance? Is there no one under trial

---

43 Bayhaqi, *Shuab al-iman*, ed. Zaghlul 3:382 #3835.
44 Tirmidhi, Ahmad, and Ibn Majah. Tirmidhi said that he had heard that Bukhari had graded this hadith weak because some of the sub-narrators did not narrate directly from each other.

that I may relieve them? Is there not such-and-such,
is there not such-and-such,' and so forth until dawn
rises."[45]

During the first Friday of the month of Rajab, or the first
night, which are both known as the "Night of wishes" (*laylat al-raghaib*) *salat al-raghaib* is performed. Although Imam
Nawawi and al-Izz ibn Abd al-Salam disapproved of its obser-
vance as based on invalid (*batil*) evidence,[46] the *hafiz* Ibn al-
Salah disagreed and considered the performance of *Salat al-raghaib* praiseworthy. Ali al-Qari said regarding this:

> The hadith saying that prayer in the daytime
> (*salat al-nahar*) is silent (*ajma*), even if invalid (*batil*),
> has a true meaning. The same applies to the hadiths
> of the prayers mentioned concerning honored days
> and exalted nights, such as *salat al-raghaib*–the most
> famous example being the prayer of mid-Shaban–
> because the hadiths concerning them (i.e. the prayers)
> are not forged, but weak.[47]
>
> Finally, Ibn Abd al-Razzaq narrates that Ibn
> Umar said: There are five nights in which invocation
> (*dua*) is not turned back: the night of Juma, the first
> night of Rajab, the night of mid-Shaban, and the two
> nights of *id*.[48]

4.6. THE STORY OF
MALIK IBN DINAR'S REPENTANCE

Imam Ibn Qudama, the shaykh of Ibn Taymiyya and the
main *fiqh* authority in the late Hanbali school, narrates that,
when Malik ibn Dinar (d. 127, 123 or 130) was asked of the circumstances of his repentance, he said:[49]

> I was a policeman and I was given to drinking. I
> bought a beautiful slave who gave me a daughter. I
> doted over my daughter and when she began to crawl
> on all fours I grew even more fond of her. Whenever I
> put a strong drink in front of me she would come to

---

45 Ahmad and Ibn Majah. Its chain contains Ibn Abi Sabra who is weak (*daif*).
46 Nawawi, *Sharh al-muhadhdhab* and *Fatawa*.
47 Ali al-Qari, *al-Asrar al-marfua* p. 234-235.
48 Ibn Abd al-Razzaq, *Musannaf* (4:317).
49 Ibn Qudama, "Those who repented" (*Kitab al-tawwabin*). (1994 ed. p. 223-225).

me and pull me away from it, or she would spill it for me. When she was two years old she died. I became consumed with grief over her loss.

When the night of mid-Shaban came–it was the night before Friday (*juma*)–I stayed home and drank. I did not pray the Isha prayer. Then I had a dream that the Day of Judgment had begun, the Trumpet was blown, the graves gave up their dead, mankind was gathered up, and I was among them. I heard something behind me. I turned around and saw a dragon of indescribable size, blue-black, rushing for me with wide-open jaws. I fled in terror.

I passed by a shaykh dressed in spotless clothes, exuding a fragrant smell. I greeted him and he greeted me back. I said to him, 'O shaykh! Protect me from this dragon, and may Allah protect you!' The shaykh wept and said, 'I am weak and it is stronger than me, I cannot overcome it. Go quickly, perhaps Allah will grant you something that will save you from it.'

I turned and resumed my flight. I climbed up on one of the promontories of the Day of Resurrection overlooking the layers of hellfire. I looked at the horror they contained and almost fell in for fear of the dragon. But a crier cried out to me, "Go back! You are not among its inhabitants." His words stilled my fears, and I went back.

But the dragon again pursued me. I went back to the shaykh and said, 'O shaykh! I begged you to protect me from this dragon but you didn't protect me." Again he wept and said, "I am weak, but proceed to this mountain. In it are kept the deposits (*wadi*) of the Muslims. If there is a deposit (*wadia*) for you, then it will help you."

I looked and saw a round-shaped mountain of silver topped with domes of hollowed pearl and hanging drapes, and every dome had two large gates of red gold encrusted with emeralds and pearls and overhung with drapes of silk.

When I saw the mountain I fled to it with the dragon in hot pursuit. As I approached the mountain one of the angels cried, 'Raise up the veils, open the gates, and look out! Perhaps this wretched one has a deposit with you that will save him from his enemy.' At this the veils were lifted, the gates were opened, and out of the palaces came children with faces like full moons. The snake was catching up to me and I was near despair.

One of the children cried, Woe to you! Come and see, all of you! His enemy is very near him.' Whereupon the children came one wave after another, and among them was the dear daughter of mine that had died two years before. When she saw me she wept and said, 'My father, by Allah!' Then she leapt in a carriage of light and came near me with the speed of an arrow. She put her left hand in my right hand and I held on to her. Then she stretched her right hand towards the dragon and it turned around and fled.

My daughter bade me sit, then she sat in my lap and began to stroke my beard and said, 'O my father! Has not the time come for those who believe, that their hearts become humble at the remembrance of Allah?' (57:16) I began to weep and said, 'O my daughter, you children know the Quran?' She replied, 'My father! We know it better than you.'

I said to her, 'Tell me about the dragon that wanted to destroy me.' She said, 'Those were the evil deeds that you built up and strengthened, and they wanted to take you to hellfire.' I asked, 'What about the shaykh I passed by?' She replied, 'O my father, those were your righteous deeds; you made them weak until they were no match for your evil deeds.'

I said, 'O my daughter! What are you all doing in this mountain?' She said, 'We are the children of Muslims, we have been given this dwelling until the Hour rises. We await whatever you send to us, and we intercede for you.' Malik said, 'Then I awoke in a start and saw that morning had come. I flung the potion from me and shattered the drinking-cups, and I repented to Allah.'

4.7. WELCOMING THE MONTH OF RAMADAN (*ISTIQBAL SHAHR RAMADAN*)[50]

Anas said that just before the month of Ramadan came, the Prophet (ﷺ) said, "Glory to Allah! If you knew what you are facing now! If you knew what is coming ahead!" Umar ibn al-

50 All the hadiths narrated in this chapter can be found in the chapter on Ramadan in Bayhaqi's *Shuab al-iman*.

Khattab said, "My father's life be ransom for you, and my mother's! O Prophet (🕮) of Allah, what is it? Did you receive revelation, or is an enemy coming?" He replied, "No, but the month of Ramadan has come, in which Allah forgives all the people of this Community."

The Prophet (🕮) also said, "If Allah's servants knew what Ramadan was, they would have wished it lasted for the whole year."

The month of Ramadan, when the Quran was revealed, is a time of tremendous blessings, and the gate of repentance and return to Allah. The Prophet (🕮) also said, "The month of Ramadan has come to you, a blessed month for the duration of which Allah has prescribed fasting for you. In it the gates of the heaven are open and the gates of hell are shut." Another version adds, "And devils are put in chains."

The Prophet (🕮) named fasting "the poor-tax of the body" (*zakat al-jasad*) and "a shield" (*junna*) from the fire. He named restraint "half of the fast" (*al-sabru nisfu al-sawm*) and "pure light" (*al-sabru diya*). When asked who were the wanderers in the verse: *Those that turn to Allah in repentance; that serve Him, and praise Him; that wander in devotion to His cause (al-saihun); that bow down and prostrate themselves in prayer; that enjoin good and forbid evil; and observe the limits set by Allah . . .* (9:112), the Prophet (🕮) explained, "The wanderers in the cause of Allah are those who fast" (*hum al-saimun*). The Prophet (🕮) also said, "There is no conceit in fasting."

The month of Ramadan is a tremendous witness on the Day of Judgment, and the Prophet (🕮) said, "I declare myself clear of them whose prosecutor is Ramadan." It brings immense rewards as he said, "Those who fast the month of Ramadan believing (in Allah and His Messenger) and seeking a reward, all their past sins are forgiven." Another version adds, "and pray (the voluntary night-prayer) in it" and in the end, "he comes out of his sins as on the day his mother gave birth to him."

Every good deed during Ramadan carries more weight than at any other time, but in particular the deed of giving. Ibn Abbas said, "The Prophet (🕮) was the most generous of people, and he was at his most generous in Ramadan." When Anas asked "What is the best charity (*sadaqa*)?" the Prophet (ﷺ) replied, "A gift in Ramadan (*sadaqatun fi ramadan*)."[51]

According to the Companion Ubada ibn al-Samit, the Prophet (ﷺ) used to say at the beginning of this month: "*Allahumma sallimni li ramadana wa sallim ramadana wa sallimhu minni mutaqabbilan* (O Allah, greet me and preserve me for Ramadan; greet and preserve Ramadan; and greet and preserve Ramadan on my behalf, and grant me its acceptance)."

The following is a traditional address of welcome recited by some scholars upon entering Ramadan.

Transliteration:

audhu billahi min al-shaytan al-rajim
bismillah al-rahman al-rahim
marhaban ahlan wa sahlan ya shahra ramadan
marhaban ahlan wa sahlan ya shahr al-quran
marhaban ahlan wa sahlan ya shahr al-nur
marhaban ahlan wa sahlan ya shahr al-ijtima
marhaban ahlan wa sahlan ya shahr al-fuqara
marhaban ahlan wa sahlan ya shahr al-tawbati wa al-ruju
marhaban ahlan wa sahlan ya shahr al-duai wa al-wuquf
marhaban ahlan wa sahlan ya shahr al-fuqarai wa al-duafa
marhaban ahlan wa sahlan ya shahr al-ihsan
marhaban ahlan wa sahlan ya shahr al-usat
marhaban ahlan wa sahlan ya shahr al-fawzi wa al-falah
marhaban ahlan wa sahlan ya shahr al-munajati wa al-tasbih
marhaban ahlan wa sahlan ya shahr al-dawati wa al-irshad
marhaban ahlan wa sahlan ya shahr al-tarawiha wa al-qiyam
marhaban ahlan wa sahlan ya shahr al-masabiha wa al-qanadil
marhaban ahlan wa sahlan ya shahr al-khazaini wa al-kunuz
marhaban ahlan wa sahlan ya shahr al-malaikati wa al-salam
marhaban ahlan wa sahlan ya shahr al-iftari wa al-suhur
marhaban ahlan wa sahlan ya shahr al-mutheerati wa al-asabb
marhaban ahlan wa sahlan ya shahr al-duafa
marhaban ahlan wa sahlan ya shahr al-ajri wa al-jaza

---

51 Tirmidhi narrated it with a good chain from Imam Bukhari and he said it is *gharib* (rare).

marhaban ahlan wa sahlan ya shahr al-sabri wa al-siyam
marhaban ahlan wa sahlan ya shahr al-saada
marhaban ahlan wa sahlan ya shahr al-miftah
marhaban ahlan wa sahlan ya shahr al-wasli wa al-wisal
marhaban ahlan wa sahlan ya shahr al-wadadi wa al-mahab-
  ba
marhaban ahlan wa sahlan ya sayyid al-shuhur
lam narif qadraka wa lam nahfaz hurmataka ya shahr al-
  ghufran
fa ardi anna wa la tashku minna ila al-rahman
wa kun shahidan lana bi al-fadli wa al-ihsan

Translation:
I seek refuge in Allah from the accursed Satan
In the name of Allah the Merciful the Beneficent
Greetings and welcome O month of Ramadan
Greetings and welcome O month of the Quran
Greetings and welcome O month of light
Greetings and welcome O month of gathering
Greetings and welcome O month of the poor
Greetings and welcome O month of repentance and return
Greetings and welcome O month of invocation and standing in
  supplication
Greetings and welcome O month of the poor and the weak
Greetings and welcome O month of doing one's best
Greetings and welcome O month of the sinners
Greetings and welcome O month of victory and success
Greetings and welcome O month of intimate discourse and glo-
  rification
Greetings and welcome O month of the call and the guidance
Greetings and welcome O month of rest-between prayers and
  standing to pray
Greetings and welcome O month of lamps and lights
Greetings and welcome O month of coffers and treasures
Greetings and welcome O month of angels and safety
Greetings and welcome O month of breaking fast and eating
  before the fast
Greetings and welcome O month of tilling and of deafness to sin

Greetings and welcome O month of the weak
Greetings and welcome O month of repayment and reward
Greetings and welcome O month of fast and patience
Greetings and welcome O month of felicity
Greetings and welcome O month of the key
Greetings and welcome O month of union and reunion
Greetings and welcome O month of friendship and love
Greetings and welcome O master of all months
We have not treated you according to your immense price
Nor truly sanctified you, O month of forgiveness,
But be pleased with us nevertheless, do not blame before the
   Merciful,
And testify for us with grace and goodness!

The great Indian poet Iqbal said about fasting:

> Fasting makes an assault upon hunger and
>   thirst.
> And breaches the citadel of sensuality . . .
> Almsgiving causes love of riches to pass away
> And makes equality familiar;
> It fortifies the heart with righteousness,
> It increases wealth and diminishes fondness for
>   wealth.
> All this is a means of strengthening thee:
> Thou art impregnable, if thy Islam be strong.
> Draw might from the litany "O Almighty One!"
> That thou mayst ride the camel of thy body.

5. ISLAMIC MALE DRESS AND THE IMPORTANCE OF THE TURBAN

5.1. INTRODUCTION

Mainstream Muslim scholars who insist on traditional (*sunna*) dress have come under criticism for stressing it in the present day and age. Is traditional (*sunna*) dress an indifferent and unnecessary aspect of Arabic culture and a tradition that carries no reward in religion?

What is the explanation of mainstream Islamic scholars on these issues in general, and in particular, with respect to the turban, white *kufi, jubba*, loose clothes, etc.?

What is the position of Nawawi on the hadith of the Prophet (ﷺ) condemning those who adopt un-Islamic clothing?

What is the position of Ibn Taymiyya on the hadith of Umar ordering Muslims in non-Arab lands not to adopt the clothing of non-Muslims?

What is the position of Maulana Ashraf Ali Thanvi on the issue of male dress?

5.2. IT IS REPREHENSIBLE (*MAKRUH*) NOT TO COVER THE HEAD IN PRESCRIBED PRAYER (*SALAT*)

It is reprehensible for a man not to cover the head in prayer if one is able to do so, as it is part of the excellence of adornment that Allah ordered when He said, *"O Children of Adam! Wear your beautiful apparel at every time and place of prayer"* (7:31). If one cannot afford a shirt or a head-cover, he may pray without them. If he can afford them, and still does not wear them, he is neglecting to obey Allah in this verse, and to heed the Prophet (ﷺ) in the hadith, "Allah likes to see the mark of His benevolence on His servant."[1] As for those who lead prayer and *khutba* in Western-style pants and other tight-fitting garments, both they and those who follow them are behaving indecently and ignorantly, jeopardizing their worship, ignoring the excellent example of the Prophet (ﷺ), and instead following the model of non-believers.

Wearing the *jilbab, izar* (loin-wrap), *thawb* (long cloth), *imama* (turban),[2] *jubba* (coat or mantle), *sirwal* (baggy pants), and so forth, is the Prophet's *sunna* of dress. There is no such thing as an unimportant or unnecessary *sunna*. It should be remembered that no *sunna* is abandoned except an innovation (*bida*) is adopted in its place. The Prophet (ﷺ) said:

> Whoever gives life to one of my *sunna*s that was eliminated after my time will receive the reward of all those who practice it without their reward being diminished . . .[3]

> Whoever gives life to one of my *sunna*s loves me, and whoever loves me is with me.[4]

> The keeper of my *sunna* at the time when my Community has lapsed into corruption will receive the reward of a martyr.[5]

Abu Hurayra narrates the following hadith:[6]

> The Prophet (ﷺ) came to the graveyard and said, 'Peace be upon you, O abode of a people of believers! We shall certainly join you, if Allah wills. How I long to see my brothers!' They said, 'O Messenger of Allah,

---

1 Al-Hakim and Tirmidhi (*hasan*).

2 Not to be confused with the *araqiyya* or "perspiration-cap," the small white cap nowadays called *taqiyya* and meant to be worn under the *qalansuwa* and *imama*, not instead of them.

3 Tirmidhi (*hasan*), Book of Knowledge; al-Baghawi, *Sharh al-sunna* 1:233.

4 Tirmidhi (*hasan gharib*), Book of Knowledge.

5 Al-Mundhiri, *al-Targhib* 1:87; al-Hakim.

6 In Muslim, Nasai, Malik, and Ahmad.

are we not your brothers?' He replied, 'You are my
Companions! As for my brothers, they are those who
have not yet appeared.' They said, 'How will you rec-
ognize those of your Community who had not yet
appeared (in your time), O Messenger of Allah?' He
replied, 'Suppose a man had horses with shiny white
marks on their foreheads and legs; would he not rec-
ognize them among other horses that are all black?'
They said, 'Yes, O Messenger of Allah!' He continued,
'Verily, they (my brothers) shall be coming with shiny
bright foreheads and limbs due to their ablutions, and
I shall lead them to my pond.'

This is not to say that religion consists only of externals.
The fact is that the Prophet (ﷺ), his Companions, the
Successors, and the pious after their time until ours, have all
worn the turban, the beard, and the loose-fitting clothes asso-
ciated with Islam. Al-Munawi said, "The turban is a *sunna*,
especially for prayer and for self-beautification, because of the
many narrations concerning it."[7] Muslims cannot condone
abandoning any of these aspects of the religion under the pre-
text that they concern externals or customs, or that they belong
to "the past," nor should they oppose those who are faithful to
each and every aspect of the *sunna*, including the Prophet's
manner of dressing, eating, and everyday living. Consider the
telling example of the Companion Abd Allah ibn Umar, who
used to dismount in order to walk on the exact same spot the
Prophet (ﷺ) had stepped, although to do so was not required by
the Prophet's law.[8]

Some "Salafis" claim, "The wearing of a hat or white clothes
or *izar* or *jilbab* is not an act of worship, and is therefore not
one of acts of *ibada* to get *hasanat*." They are incorrect since it
is an act of worship when the intention is to please Allah, and
it earns even more reward when it follows the *sunna* of the
Prophet (ﷺ), even if only in the details of his dress. Nawawi
said, in his commentary on the hadith "Actions are only according to intentions":

Whoever feeds his animal intending thereby obe-

7 Al-Munawi, Commentary on Tirmidhi's *al-Shamail*.
8 Bayhaqi, *al-Sunan al-kubra* 5:245; Ibn al-Athir, *Usd al-ghaba* 3:341; Dhahabi,
Siyar alam al-nubala 3:213; al-Qalaji, *Mawsuat fiqh ibn Umar* p. 52.

dience to Allah's order, he is rewarded, whereas if by feeding it he intends only to preserve his income, there is no reward. Al-Qarafi mentioned it.[9] Excepted from the latter case is the mount of the fighter in the way of Allah if he bridled it for that intention; if it drinks at a time he does not intend to give it drink, he will still obtain reward for it, as mentioned in Bukhari's *Sahih*.[10] Similarly in interacting with one's wife, closing the door, and extinguishing the lamps before sleep; if one intends by these acts obedience to Allah's order he will be rewarded, and if he intends something else, he will not . . .

Intention was made a legal category in order to distinguish acts of habit from acts of worship, and in order to distinguish the standing of one act of worship from that of another. An illustration of the former distinction is the act of sitting in a mosque; its purpose could be to rest according to habit, or it could be worship with the intention of seclusion and devotion (*itikaf*). The distinguishing factor here between habit and worship is intention.

Nawawi's explanation of intention makes it clear that a Muslim's wearing *sunna* attire in prayer and outside prayer is worship, that it constitutes a great *hasana*, and that it carries reward when done with the intention of obeying Allah and His Prophet (ﷺ), and following the example of the Prophet (ﷺ).

The proof that following the Prophet's example in the finest details of dress is a *sunna* is given by the following hadith:

> Narrated Ibn Umar: The Prophet (ﷺ) wore a gold ring and then the people followed him and wore gold rings too. Then the Prophet (ﷺ) said, 'I had this golden ring made for myself. He then threw it away and said, "I shall never put it on." Thereupon the people also threw their rings away.'[11]

The very least that has been said by the scholars of Sharia in the matter is that following the Prophet (ﷺ) in matters of dress, or in everyday matters such as eating, walking, and sleeping, is a matter of excellence (*ihsan*) and perfection

9 Ahmad ibn Idris al-Sanhaji al-Qarafi (626/1228-684/1285), an exact contemporary of Nawawi and like him an Ashari jurist and hadith scholar.

10 Bukhari, Book of *Jihad* #45.

11 English translation of Bukhari, Volume 9, Book 92, Number 401.

(*kamal*), is desirable (*mustahabb*), and part of one's good manners in Religion (*adab*). Every desirable practice performed with good intention earns a higher degree in Paradise for the person who performs it, than that attained by the person who neglects it.

Ibn Rajab al-Hanbali said, in his book on love of Allah and love of the Prophet (ﷺ):[12]

> Love for the Prophet (ﷺ) is on two levels: The first level is obligatory. This is the love that requires one to accept whatever the Prophet (ﷺ) brought from Allah and to receive it with love, pleasure, esteem and submission, without seeking guidance from any other source whatsoever . . . The second level is superior. This type of love requires following his example in an excellent way and fulfilling the following of his *sunna* with respect to his behavior, manners, voluntary deeds, superogatory actions, eating, drinking, dressing, excellent behavior with his wives and other aspects of his perfect manners and pure behavior. It also includes learning about his life and days. It also includes the heart trembling when mentioning him, saying prayers and blessings upon him often out of love for him, esteem for him and respect for him. It also includes loving to listen to his words and preferring them over the words of the rest of creation. And one of the greatest aspects of this love is to follow him in his abstinence of this world, to suffice with little, and to desire and pine after the everlasting hereafter.

The Prophet (ﷺ) said, "Pray as you see me pray," and there is no proof whatsoever that he ever prayed bare-headed. Rather, according to a hadith in Bukhari, the Prophet (ﷺ) wore his turban so continuously that he wiped on top of it during ablution in order not to have to remove it.[13] He wore it in war and in the *khutba*, and he received it as a gift, as established by the following three hadith:

Jabir said, "The Prophet (ﷺ) entered Makka on

---

12 Ibn Rajab al-*Hanbali*, *Istinshaq nasim al-uns min nafahat riyad al-quds* (Inhaling the breeze of intimacy from the whiffs of the gardens of sanctity).
13 Bukhari, Book of Ablution, hadith of Jafar ibn Amr's father. Chapter entitled,

the day of victory wearing a black turban and he loosened its two ends between his shoulders."[14]

Jafar ibn Amr narrates from his father, "I saw the Prophet (🕮) on the pulpit wearing a black turban with the extremity loosened between his shoulder-blades."[15]

Abu Said al-Khudri reported that when the Prophet (🕮) got a new piece of garment, he would mention it, whether a turban or a shirt or a cloak, saying, "O Allah, all praise and thanks be to You. You have given me this garment. I seek from You its good and the good that is made of it and I seek Your refuge against its evil and the evil that it is made of."[16]

The assertion of the author of *Fiqh al-sunna* is not acceptable. He states, in response to the evidence cited here, "There is no evidence whatsoever that it is preferred to cover one's head while praying."[17] This author mentions the narration, by Ibn Asakir from Ibn Abbas, that the Prophet (🕮) would sometimes remove his cap and place it in front of him as a prayer-barrier (*sutra*). However, he cites neither the *isnad* of that narration, nor its grading, nor its exact location in the works of Ibn Asakir, who is known to include all kinds of narrations. Therefore it does not constitute evidence as he presents it.

It is ironic that *Fiqh al-sunna* elsewhere mentions, among the "permissible acts in prayer," "prostrating upon one's clothing or headdress due to some excuse," which is based on the report by Ibn Abbas that the Prophet (🕮) prayed in one gar-

---

"Wearing Turbans."

14 Muslim and Abu Dawud. The first part is also in Tirmidhi (*hasan*), Ibn Majah, and Nasai. Qari said in *Jam al-wasail fi sharh al-shamail*: Some of the *ulama* have concluded from this hadith that it is permissible to wear black, although the Prophet said: "Your best garments are the white ones." Jazari said, "Black indicates the religion which does not change, like black does not change, as opposed to other colors." However, when al-Rashid asked Imam al-Awzai about wearing black he said: "It is disliked [this is Ghazali's opinion also], because the bride does not rejoice in it, the pilgrim does not wear it for *talbiya*, and the dead are not buried in it." Nawawi said: "The hadith shows that it is permitted in the *khutba*, although white is better." End of al-Qari's comments.

15 Muslim, Tirmidhi, Abu Dawud, Nasai, and Ibn Majah.

16 Abu Dawud and Tirmidhi: *Allahumma, laka al-hamd, anta kasawtanih, as aluka khayrahu wa khayra ma sunia lahu, wa audhu bika min sharrihi wa sharri ma ma sunia lah.*

17 *Fiqh al-sunna*, section entitled "Prayer prerequisites."

ment and covered his face with a portion of it to avoid the heat or coldness of the ground.[18] Then Sayyid Sabiq added, "It is disliked if it is done without any genuine reason." One wonders why he did not say the same in respect to the weaker evidence he cited to support the indifference of praying without headdress.

Fiqh al-sunna concludes the short section on praying bareheaded with another error; it reads, "According to the Hanafis, one can pray with his head uncovered. In fact they prefer this if it is done out of a sense of humility and awe." The translator of *Fiqh al-sunna* adds:

> May Allah reward Sabiq for explicitly mentioning the position of the Hanafis on this question. I have met many misinformed Muslims who insist on covering their heads in prayer because (they claim) they are following the Hanafi school of thought. (J.Z.)![19]

The following is the actual position of the Hanafi school of *fiqh*:

> According to the Hanafi school [among] the disliked acts (*al-makruhat*) in prayer are: . . . *itijar*, which is to tie a scarf around the head and leave the center bare; . . . [or] praying bareheaded out of laziness. As for praying bareheaded out of humility and submission, it is permitted (*jaiz*) and not disliked.[20]

It is strange that Sayyid Sabiq should change the Hanafi school's ruling from "disliked" to "permitted," and from "permitted" to "preferred," and it is even stranger that his translator should praise him for this error and not correct it. Even worse is the translator's labeling of Hanafi Muslims who insist on covering their heads as "misinformed."

Other "Salafis" hold a position that completely conforms with Hanafis and the rest of mainstream Islamic scholars on this topic. Following is a *fatwa* from a Hanafi/Hanbali perspective, followed by two *fatawa* from a "Salafi" perspective:

18 Imam Ahmad's *Musnad* with a sound chain.
19 Jamal al-Din Zarabozo.
20 Al-Jaziri, *al-Fiqh ala al-madhahib al-arbaa*, Kitab al-salat p. 280-281.

HANAFI/HANBALI

To go about bare-headed without a legal excuse or
a legal reason is obviously a disapproved habit. It is .
. . the custom of the transgressors (*fussaq*). It is legally abominable [*makruh*]; it is necessary [*wajib*] to
abstain from it.

Shaykh Abd al-Qadir Jilani, says: To uncover the
head or such parts of the body as are not included in
the *satr* (parts of the body that should be kept covered), though it is the method or habit of orthodox or
civilized virtuous men to keep them covered, before
people is abominable.[21]

Ibn al-Jawzi writes, "It is not hidden from a wise man that
it is abominable to keep the head bare before the people; an act
which is looked down upon and is against gentleness, human-
ness, etiquette, and gentlemanly decorum."[22]

"SALAFI"

It is permissible for a man to pray bare-headed . .
. but it is desirable (*yustahabb*) that a worshipper be
in the most perfect attire that befits him, of which the
headcovering is a part—with a turban (*imama*), a turban-cap (*qalansuwa*), or an under-cap (*kimma,
taqiyya, araqiyya*) and the like. To uncover the head
without a valid excuse is therefore reprehensible
(*makruh*), especially in the obligatory prayer, and
especially in congregation . . . but it is only reprehensible, and it is still valid, as al-Baghawi and many
others have said.[23] For the common people to disallow
themselves from praying behind a bareheaded man is
therefore incorrect, although the imam is the first of
the worshippers in whom the conditions of completion
and perfection should be met. He should be the most
scrupulous in adhering closely to the *sunna* of the
Prophet (ﷺ).[24]

In my opinion, to pray bareheaded is reprehensible, because all acknowledge that it is desirable for
the Muslim to enter prayer in the most perfect Islamic
appearance due to the hadith, "Allah is worthier of
your self-adornment" [*hasan*]. And it is not part of

---

21 Shaykh Abd al-Qadir Jilani, *Ghunyat al-talibin* 1:14.
22 Abdul Rahim Lajpuri, *Fatawa rahimiyya* 3:202 #308.
23 cf. Nawawi, *al-Majmu* 2:51.
24 Mashhur ibn Hasan Salman, *al-Qawl al-mubin fi akhta al-musallin* (p. 58-60).

excellent attire in the custom of the Salaf to habitual-
ly bare one's head, and walk in that guise on the road
and enter places of worship. Rather, it is a foreign
custom that infiltrated many Islamic countries at the
time the disbelievers invaded them and brought their
habits with them. The Muslims began to imitate
them in this, and they lost thereby their Islamic per-
sonality as well as through other similar acts . . . Nor
is it established that the Prophet (ﷺ) ever prayed
bareheaded and without a turban other than in the
state of *ihram*, although there were plenty of occasions to report it if he did. Therefore, whoever claims
that he did, let him produce the proof, for truth is
more deserving to be followed.[25]

Another aberrant view takes the fact that covering the
head is "merely a *sunna*" as an excuse not to do it. It is true
that covering the head is not *fard*, but it is a strong *sunna*. Ibn
Abidin stated that to leave a *sunna*, and belittle or disparage
it, is *kufr*.[26] One should not belittle a *sunna*. Allah says, "*Say
(O My Prophet (ﷺ) to the believers), If you love Allah, follow me*"
(3:31). A person who does not follow a *sunna*, just because it is
not *fard*, although he could adhere to it, is not acknowledging
this *ayat* and shows a lack of love for Allah.

Statements like "after all, it is (only) *sunna*," show a lack of
love for the Prophet (ﷺ), which is itself a sign of weak *iman*
(belief). Prophet Muhammad (ﷺ) says, "No one's belief is perfect until he loves me more than his parents, his children and
all mankind."

The Prophet (ﷺ) gave many instructions concerning self-
adornment and beautification for prayer, and for mere social
interaction. This is shown by the following three hadith, which
are even cited by Sayyid Sabiq:

> The Prophet (ﷺ) said, "What is the harm if any of
> you can (afford to) wear two garments for the Friday
> prayer besides the two garments he wears for his
> daily work?"[27]

25 Albani, *al-Din al-khalis* (3:214) and *al-Ajwiba al-nafia an al-masail al-waqia*
(p. 110).

26 Ibn Abidin, *Radd al-muhtar.*

27 Abu Dawud with a sound chain (Book of Friday Prayer) and Malik in the
Muwatta, Book of the call to prayer. Malik also narrates that Abu Hurayra was asked
whether a man may pray in one garment and he said "Yes, I pray in one garment while
my clothes are on the clothes-rack."

Ibn Abi al-Ahwas said: I came in shabby clothes to see the Prophet (ﷺ) and he said, "Do you have money?" I said yes. He said, "From where does your money come?" I said, "Allah has given me camels and sheep and horses and slaves." He said, "Then if Allah gave you money and possessions, let show the mark of His benevolence to you (on your person)."[28]

Abu al-Darda said that the Prophet (ﷺ) said, "You are coming to your brethren, therefore mend your mounts and mend your garments until you stand out among the people (due to your excellence) like a mole on the face. Verily, Allah does not like obscene speech nor obscene behavior."[29]

The meaning of these hadiths is that Muslims must be conspicuous in their fine appearance during and outside prayer, as well as in their excellent manners, ethics, and religion. Ibn Qudama wrote in his *Mughni* in the chapter on the characteristics of prayer:[30]

Concerning clothing there are four parts: what is permitted, what is meritorious, what is offensive, and what is forbidden. What is permitted is to wear a single garment that covers one's *awra*, or private parts, and to throw one end of it over one's shoulder . . . What is meritorious is to pray in two garments or more. By doing that, one does one's best to cover oneself appropriately. It is related (by Abu Dawud and others) that Umar said:

If Allah has enriched you, then act accordingly. Let a man dress up in his garb. Let him pray in a loinwrap (*izar*) and mantle (*burd*), in a loinwrap and shirt (*qamis*), in a loinwrap and long sleeves (*quba*), in trousers (*sarawil*) and a cloak (*rida*), in trousers and a shirt, in trousers and long sleeves, or in shorts (tubban) and a shirt.[31] . . .

Al-Tamimi said, "The single garment in prayer is

28 Narrated with a sound chain by Abu Dawud in the Book of Garments and al-Nasai in the Book of Ornaments. Ahmad narrates something similar in his *Musnad*.

29 Narrated with a sound chain by Abu Dawud in the Book of Garments and Ahmad in his *Musnad*.

30 Ibn Qudama, *Mughni* in the chapter on the characteristics of the prayer.

31 Bukhari, Book of Prayer (cf. English version vol. 1, Bk. 8, #361): Narrated Abu Hurayra: A man stood up and asked the Prophet about praying in a single garment. The Prophet said, "Has everyone of you two garments?" A man put a similar question

permitted, two is better, and four is more perfect: a shirt, trousers, a turban, and a loinwrap" . . . Al-Qadi said:

This (the desirability of self-beautification in prayer) is ascertained more for the imam than for the rest, because he is in front of those who follow the prayer, and their prayer is dependent upon his.[32]

Ibn Hajar commented on the hadith of Umar thus:

There is in the hadith (of Umar in Abu Dawud) a proof for the obligation of praying in more than one garment because praying in one garment was only done because of a lack of clothes. Also in the hadith is the proof that prayer in two garments is preferable to prayer in a single one. Qadi Iyad even declared there was no disagreement on the question. However, the expression used by Ibn al-Mundhir might suggest that there was, since when he mentioned that the Imams permitted prayer in a single garment he said, "Some of them said it was desirable to pray in two."[33]

A good illustration of all the above was given by Imam Abu Hanifa, who was famous for dressing extremely well, and perfuming and grooming himself especially for prayer, since it is a time of intimate conversation with Allah. This is the school of al-Hasan ibn Ali concerning prayer; Sayyid Sabiq also relates that when al-Hasan prayed, he would wear his best clothes. He was asked about that and he said, "Verily, Allah is beautiful and He loves beauty, so I beautify myself for my Lord." It is unimaginable that al-Hasan or Abu Hanifa's understanding did not necessitate wearing a headcover, especially considering al-Nadr's report that Abu Hanifa possessed no less than seven turban caps (*qalansuwas*).[34]

---

to Umar whereupon he replied: "When Allah makes you wealthier then you should act wealthier. Let a man gather up his clothes about himself. One can pray in a loinwrap and mantle, or a loinwrap and shirt, or in a loinwrap and long sleeves, or in trousers and a cloak, or in trousers and a shirt, or in trousers and long sleeves, or in legless breeches and long sleeves, or in shorts and a shirt." The narrator added: "And I think he said: "Or in shorts and a cloak."

32 Ibn Qudama, *al-Mughni* (1994 ed.) 1:404-405.
33 Ibn Hajar, *Fath al-bari* (1989 ed.) 1:627.
34 Narrated by Haytami his *al-Khayrat al-hisan* p. 56.

Al-Khatib al-Baghdadi narrates that one time, Abu Hanifa asked a man who was shabbily dressed to stay behind after the others had left his circle of study. He told him, "Lift up the prayer-rug and take the money that is there and buy yourself some nice clothes." The man told him he was wealthy and had no need of the money. Then Abu Hanifa said, "Has it not reached you that the Prophet (ﷺ) said Allah likes to see the mark of His benevolence on His servant?"[35]

Bukhari also narrates that Hasan al-Basri said that, in the time of the Prophet (ﷺ), because of scorching heat, "People used to prostrate on their turban-cloth (*imama*) and turban-cap (*qalansuwa*) with their hands in their sleeves." He narrates that Anas Ibn Malik said:

> We used to pray with the Prophet (ﷺ) and some of
> us used to place the ends of their clothes at the place
> of prostration because of scorching heat.[36]

The noble Companions of the Prophet (ﷺ) were wearing head-covers and long sleeves even in scorching heat!

There are esthetic criteria as well, and we have been enjoined to "wear beautiful apparel at every place of prayer." It is known from the Prophet's instructions that white, for example, falls under the category of "beautiful" because he termed it "your best clothing."[37] The fact that the Prophet (ﷺ) himself often wore white in prayer can be inferred from the saying of Umar ibn al-Khattab:

> I love to see he who recites the Quran [i.e. the
> leader of the Friday prayer] wearing white.[38]

The turban has been greatly emphasized also, because there is more evidence that the Prophet (ﷺ) and the Companions wore it at all times than there is to the contrary. This is indirectly illustrated, for example, by the instruction to remove the turban in Hajj, or the permission to wipe over it in

---

35 Al-Khatib, *Tarikh Baghdad* 13:263.

36 Bukhari, in the book of *salat*.

37 Tirmidhi (*hasan sahih*), Book of Janaiz; Nasai, Book of ornaments; Abu Dawud, Tibb and Libas; Ibn Majah, Libas and Janaiz; *Musnad Ahmad*; and Tabarani 12:65.

38 Narrated by Malik in the Book of Friday Prayer in his *Muwatta.*

wudu. It is the preferred head dress for scholars in particular; they used to be called *al-muammamun* or "the turbaned ones." It is said that Nawawi possessed only a *thawb* (long shirt) and a turban his whole life.[39]

The reports cited by Ibn al-Jawzi and Ibn al-Qayyim about the handsomeness of Hasan al-Basri have already been cited. They are presented here again, with special attention to what constituted his handsomeness:

> A group of women went out on the day of *id* and went about looking at people. They were asked, "Who is the most handsome person you have seen today?" They replied, "It is a shaykh wearing a black turban." They meant Hasan al-Basri.[40]

> Al-Hasan left behind a white cloak (*jubba*) made of wool which he had worn exclusively of any other for the past twenty years, winter and summer, and when he died it was in a state of immaculate beauty, cleanness, and quality.[41]

Both Nawawi and Ghazali recommended wearing the turban, at least on Fridays, from the time one goes out to attend Juma to the time one comes back home, especially the imam himself.[42]

Furthermore, the *sunna* of dress ensures that Muslims fulfill the sharia requirements to cover nakedness and dress modestly during both prayer and social interaction. The closer-fitting western dress often does not meet these requirements—especially men's trousers, which are usually cut too tight.

Thus it is *mandub*, or praiseworthy, to pray wearing "three of one's best clothes– shirt, trousers, and turban or cap" according to Hanafi *fiqh*;[43] "an ankle-length shirt and a turban"

---

39 See the references provided by Nuh Keller in his biographical notice for Nawawi in the *Reliance of the Traveller*.

40 Ibn al-Qayyim, *Rawdat al-muhibbin* p. 225.

41 Ibn al-Jawzi, *Sifat al-safwa* 2(4):10 (#570).

42 Their views, and those of other scholars, are quoted below, in the section on the etiquette of wearing the turban.

43 Al-Shurunbali in Muhammad Abul Quasem, *Salvation of the Soul and Islamic Devotions* (London: Kegan Paul) p. 91.

according to Shafii *fiqh*;[44] and "a shirt, trousers, turban, and a loinwrap" in Hanbali *fiqh*, as we mentioned already.[45]

The following examples illustrate the importance of *sunna* dress in the hadith, and in the practice of the Salaf.

The Prophet (襍), said on the authority of Ibn Umar, "Whoso resembles a people in appearance, he is one of them."[46]

This hadith is understood in two ways: one who looks like non-Muslims is one of them, and one who looks like Muslims is one of them. Hasan al-Basri said, "If you are of coarse character, then acquire gentleness (*tahallam*); and if you are not learned, then learn (*taallam*). A person seldom imitates a certain group without becoming one of them."[47]

Abu Dawud, Tirmidhi, and Bayhaqi narrate from Rukana's son that Rukana ibn Ubayd al-Qurashi said: I heard the Prophet (襍) say, "The difference between us and the idolaters is the turbans (*al-amaim*) on top of the turban-caps (*al-qalanis*)."[48]

This hadith does not meet the criteria of authenticity. As Tirmidhi said, "Its chain of transmission is not established." This is due to the fact that three of the six narrators in the chain are unknown. The reason both he and Abu Dawud still retained it in their compilations can be gleaned from what is known of Abu Dawud's method: whenever he could find nothing better than a weak narration to include in a given chapter, which he considered important, he chose to cite the weak narration rather than allow the message to be lost to Islam. The validity of his choice to use this hadith, which is known to be weak, is confirmed by the fact that Tirmidhi also retained it. They considered it important because despite the defects in its

---

44 Al-Misri in *Reliance of the Traveller* p. 122.

45 Ibn Qudama, *al-Mughni* (1994 ed.) 1:404-405.

46 Narrated by Abu Dawud (*Libas*) and Ahmad (2:50, 2:92) with a chain which has some weakness according to Sakhawi in *al-Maqasid al-hasana*, however he states that its authenticity is verified by other narrations. Also narrated by Ibn Abi Shayba in his *Musannaf* (5:313), Ibn Hajar in *Fath al-bari* 10:274 [Dar al-Fikr ed.], and Ibn Kathir in his *Tafsir* (8:53). Iraqi said its chain is sound (*sahih*). Al-Bazzar also relates it through Hudhayfa and Abu Hurayra, Abu Nuaym through Anas, and al-Qudai relates it through Tawus, a chain which Ibn Hibban declared *sahih*. Ibn Taymiyya in his *Iqtida al-sirat al-mustaqim* (p. 82) calls Abu Dawud's and Ahmad's chain "a good chain."

47 Al-Najm al-Razi relates it from al-Askari on the authority of Humayd al-Tawil. al-Ajluni mentions it in *Kashf al-khafa* (#2436).

48 Bayhaqi, *Shuab al-iman*.

chain of transmission, its content is true and worthy of recollection. Al-Tabrizi included it in his *Mishkat al-masabih* for the same reason.

The hadith of Rukana elucidates the hadith mentioned before it, and is confirmed by the following narrations.

3 Ibn Hibban and Ahmad, on the authority of Abu Uthman wrote, "Umar's letter reached us as we were in Azerbaijan saying, 'O Utba ibn Farqad, stay away from effeminacy and the clothing of idolaters (*mushrikin*).'"[49]

Note that shaving the beard is considered effeminacy and is forbidden (*haram*) in all major schools of Islam.

Ibn Hibban's version of Umar's saying is mentioned by Ibn Taymiyya, who interprets it as an explicit prohibition for Muslims in non-Muslim countries to wear un-Islamic clothing. He writes:

> This is a prohibition on the part of Umar directed at Muslims against all that belongs to the manner of dress of non-Muslims (*mushrikun*).[50]

4 The historian and hadith master al-Turtushi relates that Abd al-Rahman ibn Ghanam said:

> When Umar ibn al-Khattab made peace with the Christians of Syria . . . we took upon ourselves an oath that . . . [among other conditions] we shall not attempt to imitate the Muslims in their dress, whether with the *qalansuwa*, the *imama*, the sandals, or parting the hair.[51]

5 Imam Nawawi was asked, "Is one's religion and prescribed prayer (*salat*) harmed if he dresses in another fashion than that of Muslims?" He answered, "It is prohibited (*yunha*) to resemble the disbelievers in appearance, whether in clothing or otherwise, because of the sound and well-known hadith concerning this; and wearing such clothing makes one's prescribed prayer incomplete (*tanqusu bihi al-salat*)."[52]

---

49 Ahmad relates it as "non-Arabs" *(ajam)*. Ibn Hibban, *Sahih*.

50 Ibn Taymiyya, *Iqtida al-sirat al-mustaqim* (1907 ed.) p. 60. This particular passage, for some reason, was left out of the English translation of the *Iqtida* entitled *Ibn Taymiyya's Struggle Against Popular Religion* (1976).

51 Al-Turtushi, *Siraj al-muluk* p. 282.

52 Nawawi, *Fatawa*.

6 It is established that turbans increase good character from the following hadith, narrated on the authority of Ibn Abbas:

> The Prophet (ﷺ) said, "*Itammu tazdadu hilman* (wear the turban and increase your good character)" (*hilm* = also "intelligence, patience").[53]

Imam Malik said:

> The turban was worn from the beginning of Islam and it did not cease being worn until our time. I did not see anyone among the People of Excellence except they wore the turban, such as Yahya ibn Said, Rabia, and Ibn Hurmuz. I would see in Rabia's circle more than thirty men wearing turbans and I was one of them, and Rabia did not put it down until the Pleiades rose (i.e. until he slept) and he used to say, "I swear that I find it increases intelligence."[54]

7 It is further established from countless narrations that the turban is the garb of the angels, and that the angels wore it at the battles of Badr, Hunayn, and Uhud:

> Concerning the verse, "Your Lord will help you with five thousand angels bearing marks (*musawwimin*)" (3:125), Ibn Abbas said, "It is said that *musawwimin* means bearing marks or wearing turbans (*mutaammimin*)."[55]
>
> Ibn Kathir relates from Ibn Abi Hatim that Ali said, 'The mark of angels on the day of Badr was

53 Narrated in Tabarani's *al-Mujam al-kabir* (1:162), Bazzar's *Zawaid*, al-Hakim's *Mustadrak* (4:193), al-Khatib al-Baghdadi's *Tarikh Baghdad* (11:394), and Ibn Asakir's *Tahdhib tarikh dimashq al-kabir* (5:178). Al-Hakim said, "The chain of transmission of this narration is sound." Al-Haytami said that Tabarani and al-Bazzar's chains contained Ubayd Allah ibn Abi Humayd, whose narrations are not retained, but that the remainder of the narrators were trustworthy (Haythami, *Majma al-zawaid* 5:119). Ibn al-Jawzi questioned its authenticity (Ibn al-Jawzi, *al-Mawduat* 3:45), and al-Dhahabi did not confirm al-Hakim, yet Suyuti did and rejected the claim that the narration was forged by citing no less than five other chains to support it, to which Ibn Iraq added a sixth (Suyuti, *al-Laali al-masnua fi al-al-Ahadith al-mawdua* 2:139; Ibn Iraq, *Tanzih al-sharia min al-ahadith al-mawdua* 2:271). Another chain adds: "And turbans are the crowns of Arabs." (See Ibn Adi's *al-Kamil fi duafa al-rijal* 6:2082 and *Kanz al-ummal* #41135-6).

54 Ibn Abi Zayd, *al-Jami fi al-sunan* (1982 ed.) p. 228.

55 This is also reported by Makhul as quoted by Ibn Kathir in his Commentary on the verse.

white wool, and their mark was also on the forehead of their horses.'[56]

Ibn Asakir and Suyuti relate, on the authority of Aisha, that the Prophet (ﷺ) said, 'Most of the angels I have seen were wearing turbans.' [57]

The following seven narrations are from Suyuti's Commentary on Quran, entitled *al-Durr al-manthur fi al-tafsir al-mathur*.

In Tabarani and Ibn Mardawayh, on the authority of Ibn Abbas with a weak chain, 'The Prophet (ﷺ) said concerning *musawwimin*: it means *muallamin* or marked.' Ibn Kathir mentions it.

On the authority of Abd Allah ibn al-Zubayr, he was wearing a yellow turban on the day of Badr, so the angels descended wearing yellow turbans.[58]

On the authority of Abbad ibn Abd Allah ibn al-Zubayr, on the day of Badr, al-Zubayr was wearing a yellow turban among the people. So the Prophet (ﷺ) said, 'The angels have descended wearing the same mark as Abu Abd Allah,' and the Prophet (ﷺ) himself came wearing a yellow turban.[59]

On the authority of Urwa and Ibn al-Zubayr, 'The day of Badr the angels came down on piebald horses, wearing yellow turbans.'[60]

On the authority of Ibn Abbas, "The mark of the angels on the day of Badr was white turbans whose ends were hanging in their backs, and on the day of Hunayn, red turbans.'[61]

In Tabari's commentary, a Companion who fought at Badr

56 Ibn Kathir, *Tafsir*.

57 Ibn Asakir, *Tahdhib* (6:232), and Suyuti, *al-Habaik fi akhbar al-malaik*

58 In Ibn Abi Shayba's *Musannaf*, Ibn Jarir al-tabari's *Tafsir*, Ibn al-Mundhir, Ibn Abi Hatim, and Ibn Mardawayh. Abu Nuaym says the same in reference to Gabriel in his book *Fadail al-Sahaba*, on the authority of Urwa. Ibn Kathir mentions that Ibn al-Zubayr was wearing *itijar*, i.e. a single covering from head to foot.

59 In Abu Nuaym and Ibn Asakir.

60 Abd al-Razzaq in his *Musannaf* and Tabari in his *Tafsir* mention this.

61 In Ibn Ishaq's *Sira* and in Tabarani, Ibn Kathir mentions it.

and Uhud, named Abu Usayd (Malik ibn Rabia al-Saidi), said to his grandson Zubayr ibn Mundhir:

> If I had my eyesight and if you came with me to Uhud, I would tell you about the mountain-pass out of which came the angels, wearing yellow turbans which they had thrown back between their shoulders.[62] Abu Usayd was the last of the Companions of Badr to die (in 60 H).

> Malik said Gabriel was seen in the image of (the Companion) Dihya (ibn Khalifa) al-Kalbi, and he was wearing a turban with its extremity hanging between his shoulder blades.[63]

It is hoped that the above presentation of evidence and mainstream Islamic scholars' views will help counter the "Salafi" innovations in respect to male dress, and put to rest the incorrect views of al-Qaradawi and other modern sources. Muslims are advised to beware of those who claim that they are reviving the *sunna*, while they discard the turban, the *jubba*, and the beard, and bring Western-style shirts, pants, and even boots into the masjid.

This chapter is concluded with a translation of Shaykh al-Islam Imam Kawthari's *fatwa* on headcoverings and footgear for men during prescribed prayer (*salat*), from his invaluable *Maqalat*.

5.3. IMAM KAWTHARI'S (D. 1371/1951) *FATWA*: ON BARING THE HEAD IN PRESCRIBED PRAYER (*SALAT*)[64]

> There has a been a spate of questioning these days on the legality of the male's doffing headcover at prayer, without excuse, and of praying in sandals. A certain type of people has sprung up who delights in criticizing the good and disseminating corruption.

---

62 Tabari, *Jami al-bayan an tawil al-Quran.* Suyuti also mentions it with a slightly different wording.

63 Ibn Abi Zayd, *al-Jami fi al-sunan* (1982 ed.) p. 229.

64 Al-Kawthari, *Maqalat* (Riyad: Dar al-ahnaf, 1414/1993) p. 201-218.

They like to surprise the masses by going against
what all have inherited from earlier generations,
from Salaf to Khalaf. These pseudo-*mujtahid*s run
after *fitna* by creating disturbances in the Houses of
Allah, among Muslims in their acts of worship. They
are the strangest of people in their mindset and the
greatest in resemblance to the Khawarij in their
magnifying small matters and making light of great
ones.[65] There is no need to tarry in describing them.
The people have realized who they are and their
endeavor to split asunder the oneness of Muslims, so
they have rejected them and their missionary work
everywhere.

As for the prayer of one who removes his head-
cover without excuse, it is valid provided it meets the
conditions and pillars of prayer, however:

•It contravenes the *sunna* transmitted from the
Prophet (ﷺ) and the practice transmitted from
Muslims to Muslims in all the lands through the centuries;
•It resembles that of the People of the Book, for
they pray, as everyone can see, bareheaded;
•It constitutes a rejection of the order for
Muslims to "*Wear your beautiful apparel at every time
and place of prescribed prayer*" (7: 31). Bayhaqi cited
in his *Sunan al-kubra* the hadith of Anas ibn Iyad
from Musa ibn Uqba from Nafi from Abd Allah [ibn
Umar], and Nafi said he thought nothing other than
that it came from the Prophet (ﷺ) himself: 'Whenever
one of you prays, let him wear two pieces of clothing,
for verily Allah is the worthiest of those for whom one
adorns oneself. If one does not have two pieces of

65 The Khawarij are from among the tribes of Banu Hanifa, Banu Tamim, and
Wail, and the Najd area of Eastern Arabia. They committed *baghi* (rebellion) against
the Caliph and opposed the larger group of Muslims. They declared both the Caliph
and Muawiya disbelievers and declared their blood and property forfeit, as well as the
blood and property of those with them. They made their land a land of war and
declared their own land an abode of faith. They only accepted from the Prophet's *sunna*
what agreed with their own doctrine, and supported their doctrine with anything
ambiguous in the Quran. They used to apply Quranic verses meant to refer to disbelievers to believers, as predicted by the Prophet (Bukhari, English ed. 9:50). Ibn Abbas
debated them until four thousand returned to the truth. They were the first to sepa-
rate from the Congregation of Muslims. The Prophet referred to them as "The dogs of
the people in Hell" (Sound (*sahih*) hadith related through various chains by Ibn Majah,
Muqaddima 12, and Ahmad 4:355, 382, 5:250, 253, 256, 269.). The Prophet gave the
order to fight and kill them by saying, "They will pass through Islam like an arrow
passes through its quarry. Wherever you meet them, kill them!" (Bukhari and Muslim
have more than one form of this hadith). Imam Ibn Abidin (d. 1252/1836) said:

clothing, let him wear the *izar* (loin-wrap) whenever he prays. Let none of you dress in the manner of the Jews.'[66]

Bayhaqi also cited the hadith of al-Abbas al-Duri, from Said ibn Amir al-Dubi, from Said ibn Abi Azuba, from Ayyub from Nafi who said:
Ibn Umar saw me pray in a single garment and he said, "Did I not give you clothes?" I said yes. He continued, "And if I sent you on an errand would you go out like this?" I said no. He said, "Then Allah is worthier of your self-adornment."

It is narrated by Tahawi in *Sharh maani al-athar* (1:221), Tabarani, Bayhaqi in his *Sunan al-kubra* (2:236), and Haythami said in *Majma al-zawaid* (2:51), "Its chain is fair (*hasan*)." Albani included it in *al-Silsila al-sahiha* (#1369).

Bayhaqi also cited the hadith of Yusuf ibn Yaqub al-Qadi, from Sulayman ibn Harb, from Hammad ibn Zayd from Ayyub, from Nafi: Umar entered my room one day as I was praying in a single garment and he said, "Don't you have two garments in your possession?" I said yes. He said, "In your opinion, if I sent you to one of the people of Madina on an errand, would you go in a single garment?" I said no. He said, "Then is Allah worthier of our self-beautification or people?"

The above illustrates the jurists' discernment in declaring blameworthy and reprehensible the performance of prayer in attire that one would not wear if he went out to see those he respects. There is no doubt that in the social practice of Muslims, from the Salaf down to the Khalaf, no-one goes bareheaded to see those he respects. Consequently praying bareheaded is disliked.

The name of *Khawarij* is applied to those who part ways with Muslims and declare them disbelievers, as took place in our time with the followers of Ibn Abd al-Wahhab who came out of Najd and attacked the Two Noble Sanctuaries (Makka and Madina). They (Wahhabis) claimed to follow the *Hanbali* school, but their belief was such that, in their view, they alone are Muslims and everyone else is a *mushrik* (polytheist). Under this guise, they said that killing Sunnis and their scholars was permissible, until Allah the Exalted destroyed them in the year 1233/1818 at the hands of the Muslim army (Imam Muhammad Ibn Abidin, *Hashiyat radd al-muhtar ala al-durr al-mukhtar*, 3:309 *Bab al-bughat* [Chapter on Rebels]).

66 Bayhaqi, *Sunan al-kubra* 2:236.

5.4. THE ETIQUETTE OF WEARING A TURBAN (*ADAB AL-IMAMA*)

The Prophet (ﷺ) ordered Abd al-Rahman ibn Awf to prepare for a military expedition on which he was sending him. The next morning the Prophet (ﷺ) was wearing a turban of black cotton. He summoned Abd al-Rahman, untied his own turban, tied it on him, and let its extremity hang loose behind him about one foot ["4 fingers" = 4 x 8 cm.] with the words, '(Wear it) like this, O Ibn Awf, it is more like the Arabs and more beautiful.' Then the Prophet (ﷺ) ordered Bilal to give him the flag. He glorified Allah then said, 'Conduct your raids for the sake of Allah and fight those who disbelieve in Allah; don't exceed limits, don't act treacherously, don't mutilate, and don't kill women. This is the pact of Allah's Messenger among you.'[67]

Tirmidhi narrates that Abd Allah Ibn Umar said when the Prophet (ﷺ) tied his turban, he would let its extremity hang between his shoulder-blades.[68]

Nafi, the narrator from Ibn Umar, adds, 'And Ibn Umar used to let the extremity of his turban hang between his shoulder-blades.'

Ubayd Allah, Umar's grandson and the narrator from Nafi, adds, 'And I saw al-Qasim (Abu Bakr's grandson) and Salim (Umar's son) do the same.'

Munawi explains Nafi's and Ubayd Allah's statements saying, 'It means that this is a strong *sunna* (*sunna muakkada*) which must be kept and the abandonment of which is unacceptable to the pious (*sulaha*).'[69]

Mubarkafuri, in his super commentary on Ibn al-Arabi's commentary on Tirmidhi, said, "This hadith indicates the preference of letting loose the turban's end between the shoulder-blades, and it appears to be fair (*hasan*).[70]

---

67 Haythami says in *Majma al-zawaid*: "Ibn Majah narrates some of it; al-Bazzar narrates it (all), and its sub-narrators are trustworthy *(thiqat)*."

68 Tirmidhi *(hasan gharib)*. Mubarkafuri said: "It appears to be fair *(hasan)*."

69 Al-Munawi, Commentary on the Chapter entitled "Concerning the Prophet's Turban" in Tirmidhi's Book *al-Shamail*.

70 Al-Mubarkafuri, *Tuhfat al-ahwadhi*, chapter on the turban.

Qari quotes Mayrak as saying, 'It has been firmly established from the *siras* with authentic narrations that the Prophet (☪) used to let the extremity of his turban hang loose between his shoulders at times, and at times did not.'[71]

Mubarkafuri cites al-Sanani as saying,[72] 'The etiquette of the turban is that one shortens the free extremity of the turban lest it reaches an indecent length . . . and lets it down between the shoulderblades, but it is permissible to leave it tucked in.'[73]

He also cites Nawawi as saying in *Sharh al-madhhab*: 'To let down the extremity of the turban exceedingly, as with a robe, is forbidden if done out of conceit and disliked if done for any other reason . . . and it is permissible to wear the turban with or without letting down its extremity; it is not disliked to wear it without doing so, and it is utterly wrong to forbid one from wearing it without doing so.'[74]

Munawi quotes Shafii's opinion whereby, 'Although the Prophet (☪) feared that letting it down could lead to conceit, yet he did not order to leave it, but to keep it and keep one's ego in check.'[75]

Qari and Munawi also quote Ibn al-Qayyim as relating that his shaykh, Ibn Taymiyya, had told him a beautiful thing; namely, that after the Prophet (☪) saw that his Lord put His hand between his shoulders, he honored that place with the extremity of the turban. This is a reference to the hadith in Tirmidhi whereby the Prophet (☪) said: 'My Lord came to me in the best image and asked over what did the angels of the higher heaven vie, and I said I did not know, so He put His hand between my shoulders, and I felt its coolness in my innermost, and the knowledge of all things came to me.'

Concerning the meaning of Tirmidhi's hadith of Rukana, whereby the Prophet (☪) said, "The difference between us and the idolaters is the turbans on top of the turban-caps," Ibn al-Jawzi says that, in the opinion of some scholars, the *sunna* is to wear both *qalansuwa* (turban-cap) and *imama* (turban), and that to wear the *qalansuwa* alone is the fashion of

---

71 Al-Qari, *Jam al-Wasail*, chapter on the turban.
72 Al-Sanani, *Subul al-salam*.
73 Al-Mubarkafuri, *Tuhfat al-ahwadhi*, chapter on the turban.
74 *Ibid.*
75 Al-Munawi, Commentary on Tirmidhi's *al-Shamail*.

non-Muslims.[76] Al-Munawi asserts that the *sunna* is attained by wearing the imama either on the head or on top of the *qalansuwa*, and that wearing the *qalansuwa* alone, even if permissible, does not fulfill the *sunna*.[77]

The hadith master and lexicographer Murtada al-Zabidi, who is the compiler of *al-Tajrid al-sarih* and *Taj al-arus*, said in his exhaustive commentary on Ghazali's *Ihya ulum al-din*:

The turban is desired (*mustahabb*) on Fridays for both the imam and the congregation. Nawawi said that it is desired for the imam, to beautify his appearance (i.e. more than everyone else), to wear the turban, and wear a *rida* (= *jubba*, a loose outer garment or robe). The application of the *sunna* consists in winding the turban on the head or on top of a qalansuwa. It is preferable to wear it large, but it is necessary to define its length and width by what fits the wearer's custom, according to his time and place. To add to this is disliked by the divine law.[78]

Suyuti was asked what the length of the Prophet's turban was and what he wore underneath it. He answered:

Al-Barizi mentions in *Tawthiq ura al-iman*[79] that the Prophet (ﷺ) used to wear the *qalansuwa* [cap] under the *imama* [turban], and he used to wear the *qalansuwa* without the *imama*, and he used to wear the *imama* without the *qalansuwa*, and he used to wear the *qalansuwa* with handles [i.e. referring to a metal helmet] during war. Very often he used to wear a *harqaniyya* or black turban on his journeys and to wear it with *itijar* [completely covered from head to foot with a single cloth], and in *itijar* one wears something underneath the turban. It is probable that it was not the turban but an *isaba* [tied head-cloth, as opposed to the *kufiyya*, which is worn loose] on his head and forehead. He had a turban that, when he tied it on, was referred to as *al-sahab* [the clouds]. He dressed Ali ibn Abi Talib with this, and when Ali

---

76 Quoted by al-Qari.

77 Al-Qari and al-Munawi, commentaries on the chapter on the Prophet's turban in Tirmidhi's *al-Shamail*.

78 Al-Zabidi, *Ithaf al-sadat al-muttaqin* 3:253.

79 Qari in *al-Mirqat* also mentions that Rawyani and Ibn Asakir relate it on the authority of Ibn Abbas.

came out the Prophet (ﷺ) would say, "Ali has come to you among the clouds," meaning that he was wearing the turban which he gave him. This is what Barizi mentions. Al-Qazzaz says that the *qalansuwa* is a *ghishaun mubattan* [lined covering] one uses to conceal the head, and Bayhaqi [also Tabarani and Qari] related from Ibn Umar that the Prophet (ﷺ) used to wear a white *qalansuwa*. All that has been said indicates that what the Prophet (ﷺ) and the Companions used to wear under the turban was the *qalansuwa*.

As for the length of the noble turban, it was not established in a hadith. Bayhaqi related in *Shuab al-iman* from Abu Abd al-Salam that the latter said, "I asked Ibn Umar, how did the Prophet (ﷺ) wear the turban?" He replied, "He used to wind the turban around his head and tuck it in the back and let its tail dangle between his shoulder-blades." This indicates that it was several arms in length, evidently around ten arm-lengths or a little bit more.[80]

Suyuti's deduction that the length of the Prophet's turban was ten arm-lengths is contested by Shawkani, who said the same action (winding, tucking, and loosening the end) could be accomplished with a turban of under three arm-lengths. Jazari said: I have perused the books and questioned the biographies and history-books in order to find out the length of the Prophet's turban, blessings and peace be upon him, and I found nothing, until I was told by someone I trust that he found something in Nawawi whereby the Prophet (ﷺ) had a short *imama* and a long *imama*, and that the short one was seven arms long and the long one ten.[81]

Qari cites Jazari then says, "It appears from the wording in *al-Madkhal* that the Prophet's turban was seven arms long exclusively, without any qualification of short or long."[82] Mubarkafuri cites all of the above opinions to conclude, "Whoever claims that the length of the Prophet's turban was such and such arm-lengths must back it up with an authentic proof, otherwise pure presumption is null and void." Munawi quotes Ibn Hajar al-Haytami as saying that all

---

80 Suyuti, *al-Hawi li al-fatawi* (Beirut: Dar al-kutub al-ilmiyya, 1395/1975) p. 72.
81 Chapter on clothing.
82 Jazari, *Tashih al-masabih*.

reports concerning the length of the Prophet's turban are baseless.

Ibn al-Qayyim and al-Qari say that wearing a very large turban exposes the head to hardship, that a small one protects neither from heat nor from the cold, and that the size of the Prophet's turban was between the two. Finally, al-Qari quotes the author of *al-Madkhal* as saying, "You must put on the *sarwal* while sitting and the turban while standing."[83]

5.5. ASHRAF ALI THANVI'S *FATWA* ON THE REQUISITES OF ISLAMIC DRESS[84]

It is essential for Muslims to be distinguished from the followers of other religions and cultures. Muslims should be recognizable by their external appearances. Outward appearance is among the prominent features of Islam, for it is through this that the identity of the nation is maintained, and Muslims are guarded against assimilation into other, non-Muslim cultures.

Islam prohibits the unnecessary adoption of the ways and appearances of other nations. Certain acts that conceal the Muslim's identity are not permissible, even if they do not belong to the special characteristics of other communities. Thus, shaving or cutting the beard, and wearing shorts that expose one's bare flesh, are completely forbidden. If a Muslim, in adopting these forbidden ways, despises or mocks the prohibitions of the Law, his transgression worsens from sin to disbelief.

There are certain things that are not exclusive to any particular community whose adoption will be permissible. If a form of dress is particular to a non-Muslim community, it will be sinful for Muslims to adopt it, even if the Law's requirement to conceal nudity is fulfilled. . . It will not be permissible to adopt the ways of non-Muslims, even if such ways have no religious undertones. If the ways adopted from the disbelievers are of religious import, it will amount to disbelief, e.g. wearing a cross, etc.

---

83 Qari, *Mirqat.*
84 Qari, *Jam al-Wasail.*

There are things that are of neither religious nor cultural import, and which are of real use and benefit. Even if such things are the inventions of the disbelievers, there will be nothing wrong in adopting them. This applies to inventions of transportation, communications, weapons, and other items of benefit. However, in such matters, the layman should not determine the permissibility or prohibition of anything. He should obtain the advice and direction of the *ulama* who will properly inform him. It is also prohibited to adopt the ways and appearances of Muslims who happen to be transgressors (*fussaq*) and innovators (*ahl al-bida*). It is also prohibited for men to take on the attire and appearance of women and vice versa.

It is very essential that Muslims adopt Islamic ways and methods in all their affairs, whether worldly or related to worship. There is great benefit for Muslims in maintaining their Islamic identity in all their affairs and not only in matters pertaining to worship. The Quran and the hadith emphasize this.

Abdullah ibn Umar narrates that the Prophet (ﷺ) said, "My *umma* will be split into seventy-three sects of which all, save one, will be in the Fire." People inquired, "Which group will be saved?" The Prophet (ﷺ) replied, "That group which will be on my path and the path of my Companions."[85]

"Path" in the context of this hadith refers to the Way that has to be followed. Following a way that opposes to it leads to hell-fire. The Prophet (ﷺ) did not restrict his Path to any specific department of the Sharia. This hadith covers both mundane and spiritual matters. Affairs pertaining to our worldly life as well as religious life are included in the Path of the Prophet (ﷺ) and that of his Companions. This is not a question that everyone can expound on the basis of his opinion. In this matter, the masses have no option other than to inquire from the *ulama*, who understand these issues. They have to follow the *ulama*. Without following the direction given by the *ulama*, the religion of the masses is not safe.

---

85 Adapted from the article "The distinguishing characteristics of the follower of Islam" published on the webpage hyperlink http://dsuper.net/~katiya/identity.htm.

would not have done it if it constituted *shirk*, or led to it.[5] This is confirmed by the *tabiin*, including Said ibn al-Musayyib, al-Dahhak, Jafar al-Sadiq, Ibn Sirin who accepted the unconditional wearing of *tawiz* by both adults and children. Furthermore, neither Malik ibn Anas,[6] Imam Nawawi, nor the narrators of Abd Allah ibn Amr's report, such as Tirmidhi, Nasai, Ahmad, or Abu Dawud had any objection to it.

Ibn Abi Zayd al-Qayrawani, an early scholar of the Maliki school, said:

> There is nothing wrong in the use of protective verses, or the use of medicine in the treatment of diseases, or the taking of drugs; blood-letting, cauterizing and cupping are all good treatments. The application of antimony to the eye for men is permissible when done for medical purposes. For women, however, it is part of make-up . . . There is no harm in cauterization or using the verses of the Quran or decent speech for cure of disease. There is no harm in wearing a pendant which contains verses of the Holy Quran."[7]

Allah said, *"And We reveal of the Quran what is a healing and a mercy for the believers, and the wrong-doers are not increased except in loss"* (17:82) Following are some of the scholars' explanations of this verse:

Al-Baydawi wrote:

> It is said that it refers to what cures from physical diseases, such as the Verses of Healing (*ayat al-shifaa*) and *Surah al-Fatiha* (the Opening Chapter)."

Al-Khazin wrote:

> With regard to the Quran being a cure for diseases of the body, this is because the blessing obtained (*tabarruk*) from its recitation protects from many (physical) diseases, as shown by the hadith of the Prophet (ﷺ) concerning *Surah Fatiha* when he said,

---

5 This narration is cited in full further down.
6 As related by Qurtubi.
7 Ibn Abi Zayd al-Qayrawani, *Risala,* a manual of *fiqh* (Chapter 44).

"How did you know that they were protective verses
(*ruqya*)?"[8]

Qurtubi wrote:

It has been said that he who does not seek cure
through the Quran, Allah does not cure him. The
scholars interpret that verse in two ways however.
The first is, that cure is for the hearts, by the removal
of ignorance and doubt which hinder the understanding of miracles and matters pointing to Allah
Almighty. The second is, that cure is for outward diseases, through the use of healing verses (*ruqya*) and
seeking refuge and the like. Bukhari and Muslim
relate the hadith of *ruqya* through Abu Said al-
Khudri."[9]

Qurtubi then lists instructions for making a kind of *ruqya*
called *nushra*; various verses are recited over a clean container
that is then filled with water. The water is then used for *wudu*
by someone who already has a valid *wudu*, and who also soaks
his head and limbs with it but does not use it for *ghusl* or *istin-
ja*. It may be drunk. He then prays two *rakats*, after which he
asks for healing. He does this for three days. Qurtubi also cites
Ibn Abd al-Barr's statement that the Prophet's condemnation of
nushra concerns whatever contradicts the Quran and *sunna*,
not what conforms to it.

Qurtubi continues:

The Prophet (ﷺ) said, "Cure for my Community is
in but three things: verses of Allah's Book, a mouthful
of honey, or cupping." He also said, "Ruqya is allowed
as long as there is no idolatry [*shirk*]; and if you can
help your brother, help him." Malik ibn Anas said, "To
hang writings of Allah's Names upon oneself is permitted for healing and blessing but not for protection
against the evil eye."[10] Abd Allah ibn Amr used to
hang a protective invocation taught by the Prophet
(ﷺ) around the necks of his young children. (Abu

8 Bukhari and Muslim.
9 A Companion healed an Arab from scorpion-bite by reciting *Surah al-Fatiha* on
him seven times and the Prophet later asked him, "How did you know it was a *ruqya?*"
10 See Abu Hayyan, *Tafsir al-bahr al-muhit* 6:74."

Dawud and Tirmidhi—*hasan*) The Prophet (ﷺ) and the Companions hated the pagan kind of *ruqya* or talisman or necklace (*tamima, qilada*). *Istishfa* or seeking blessing with the Quran is not idolatry (*shirk*), whether hung on oneself or not. Whoever cites the hadith whereby the Prophet (ﷺ) said, "Whoever hangs something (upon oneself), he is left to it for protection" (Tirmidhi, Nasai, and Ahmad, all with a weak chain), and that of Ibn Masud's removal of his wife's pendant saying, "Ibn Masud's family have no need of *shirk*" (al-Hakim and Ibn Hibban in his Sahih) . . . this was all as a prohibition of what the people of the Age of Ignorance (*jahiliyya*) used to do in wearing amulets and pendants, thinking that they protected them against calamity, whereas only Allah protects, relieves, and tests, and He has no partner. So the Prophet (ﷺ) forbade them what they used to do in their ignorance. Aisha said, "Whatever is worn after the descent of calamity is not an amulet (*laysa min al-tamaim*)." . . . As for seeking cure (*istishfa*) with the Quran whether worn on oneself or not then it is no *shirk* at all, the Prophet (ﷺ) said, "Whoever hangs something (upon oneself), he is left to it for protection." Therefore who hangs Quran is certainly taken under Allah's protection, and He will not leave him to other than Him. Wearing a *ruqya* is accepted by Ibn al-Musayyib, ad-Dahhak, Jafar as-Sadiq, and Ibn Sirin.

Bukhari narrates the hadith whereby the Prophet (ﷺ) used to seek protection (*yuawwidhu*) for al-Hasan and al-Husayn saying:

> Your father [i.e. ancestor] used to seek protection with these words for Ismail and Ishaq: '*Audhu bi kali-matillah al-tamma min kulli shaytanin wa hamma, wa min kulli aynin lamma* (I seek refuge in Allah's perfect words from every devil and every venomous animal, and from every evil eye).'[11]

Al-Khattabi mentioned that this hadith was adduced by Imam Ahmad as proof that the Quran was uncreated, since the Prophet (ﷺ) did not seek protection in anything created.[12]

---

11 Bukhari in the 10th chapter of the Book of the sayings of the Prophets (*ahadith al-anbiya*) in his *Sahih*.

12 Ibn Hajar mentioned it in *Fath al-bari* (1989 ed. 6:506).

Imam Nawawi said:

> One may adduce as evidence for their [amulets
> (*tawiz*) containing protective or healing words (*ruqya,*
> *hijab*)] permissibility the hadith of Amr ibn Shuayb,
> from his father [Abd Allah ibn Amr], from his grand-
> father [Amr ibn al-As], that the Messenger of Allah
> (Allah bless him and give him peace) used to teach
> them, for fearful situations, the words, *"Audhu bi*
> *kalimatillah al-tammat min ghadabihi wa sharri*
> *ibadihi wa min hamazat al-shayatina wa an yahdu-*
> *run* (I seek refuge in Allah's perfect words from His
> wrath, from the evil of His servants, from the whis-
> pered insinuations of devils, and lest they come to
> me)." Abd Allah ibn Amr [in Tirmidhi and Abu Dawud:
> Abd Allah ibn Umar] used to teach these words to
> those of his sons who had reached the age of reason,
> and used to write them and hang them upon those
> who had not.[13]

"*Hasan*" is one of the degrees of authenticity used by the
authorities in hadith methodology. It is used to establish or confirm correct practice by the majority of the *fuqaha*. Nawawi
said, "*Al-hasanu kal-sahih fi al-ihtijaj bihi wa in kana dunihi*
fi al-quwwa (the *hasan* is like the *sahih* in probative value even
if it does not reach its strength)."[14] This is why he retained this
narration both in his *Majmu* and in *Kitab al-adhkar*, his book
on recommended *dua*s, invocations, and related practices for
Muslims.

Imam Qasim ibn Sallam (d. 224) relates:[15]

> Hajjaj said: I asked Ata about the one who hangs
> on himself a verse or verses from the Quran, or some-
> thing to that effect? He said, "We have not heard that
> it was disliked except from you, the scholars of Iraq."

---

layla (#765), and Ahmad in his *Musnad* (2:181). Al-Tibrizi cites it in *Mishkat al-*
masabih (see Robson translation 1:527). See also the *Reliance of the Traveller* p. 880.
Nawawi included it in his *Adhkar* (Taif ed. p. 133 #307 and p. 166 #369) in the chapters entitled, "What to say if one becomes afraid in one's sleep" and "What to say if anything terrifies one." Even Albani included the hadith in his *Silsila sahiha* (#264).

  13 Nawawi, *al-Majmu sharh al-muhadhdhab* vol. 2 p. 71 (Salafiyya Publishing
House in Madina). The hadith is related in Abu Dawud (book of *tibb* #3893), Tirmidhi
who said it is *hasan gharib* (book of *daawat* #3519), al-Nasai in *Amal al-yawm wa al-*
  14 Nawawi, *al-Taqrib wa al-taysir* [Kind #2].
  15 Ibn Sallam, *Fadail al-quran* (p. 223-234 #11-13).

Mujahid and Khalid related from Abu Qilaba that they did not see any harm in it.

Shuba, from Hammad [ibn Salama], from Abraham [al-Nakhi] who said, "This is only disliked for the *junub* – the one in a state of major impurity – and the women in menses."

Shaykh Abd al-Qadir al-Gilani relates that Imam Ahmad said that during a fever he had the following verse hung upon him: *"O fire! Be coolness and safety for Abraham. And they wished to set a snare for him, but We made them the greater losers"* (21:69-70).[16]

The objection that "if *tawiz* does protect someone from the evil of the world, and was approved by the Prophet (ﷺ), then he would have hung them around his children and grandchildren's necks" is incorrect and unacceptable. It is well-known that the lawfulness of an act in Islam is not exclusively derived from the Prophet's personal performance or approval of that act. To claim otherwise is an innovation that has seemed to gain momentum recently, among people who are not competent to speak about Sharia.

A follower of mainstream Islam was asked a question about *tawiz* and his reply was forthright:

Is there a problem with hanging a calligraphic rendering of *Surah Fatiha* on the wall of your living room? Many Muslims have this hanging in their homes. I don't think they're putting their faith in these papers with ink scrawled on it, are they? I think a human being is on a higher plane than a wall, so if I hang the *Surah Fatiha* around my neck, what would the problem be? How about if I write a supplication asking Allah to protect me and hang this around my neck? Am I expecting the paper to protect me? This would be foolish. Around the Kabah in Makka there is a black covering with words embroidered on it. Are all those people circling the Kabah expecting the writing to save and protect them? Allah is the only Protector, everyone knows that. The *tawiz* is a reminder of that."

16 al-Jilani, *al-Ghunya* (al-Walid ed. 1:201).

6.3. THE "VERSES OF HEALING" IN THE QURAN

1 *"And He heals the breasts of a believing people"* (9:14). Ibn Kathir, al-Jalalayn, and Qurtubi say this verse refers to the Banu Khuzaa, according to Mujahid and Ikrima. Qurtubi says:

> The believing people in this verse are the Banu Khuzaa. The Quraysh had helped the Banu Bakr against them, and the Khuzaa were allies of the Prophet (ﷺ). A man of the Banu Bakr had recited poetry attacking the Prophet (ﷺ) and one of the Banu Khuzaa had told him, "I shall break your jaw if you repeat this." He did and he broke his jaw. A battle ensued in which many of the Banu Khuzaa were killed. Amr ibn Salem al-Khuzai and a small group went to the Prophet (ﷺ) and told him the news. The Prophet (ﷺ) entered Maymuna's house, called for water, and began to wash saying, "If the Banu Kab [Amr's tribe and the strongest element of the Banu Khuzaa] did not help me I would not have been given victory." Then he ordered for preparations to be made for the expedition to Makka, and Makka was conquered (and the Banu Khuzaa were thus given satisfaction by Allah).

2 *"O people! Advice has come from your Lord, and a cure for what is in the breasts, and a guidance and mercy for the believers"* (10:57).

> Qurtubi writes, "It means a cure for what is in the hearts of doubt, hypocrisy, disagreement, and dissension."

> Ibn Kathir says, "A cure for what is in the hearts of suspicion and doubts; it is the removal of what is in the heart of corruption and sin."

> Al-Jalalayn says, "A cure for what is in the hearts of corrupt beliefs and doubts."

> According to al-Khazin, "A cure for what is in the

hearts of the illness of ignorance, because such illness is worse for the heart than bodily sickness."

3 *"A multi-colored drink issues from their bellies, in it there is healing for people"* (16:69).

Ibn Kathir writes:

> Specialists of prophetic medicine (*tibb nabawi*) said: If He had said, "In it there is the medicine for people, it would have been a cure for all ailments." The Prophet (ﷺ) said, "Use the two medicines: honey and the Quran." (Ibn Majah; Ibn Kathir said its chain of transmission is fair). He also said, "A cure is in three things: A gulp of honey, cupping, and cauterizing; but I forbid my followers to use cauterization." (Bukhari) He also said, "If there is any healing in your medicine, then it is in cupping, a gulp of honey, or cauterization that suits the ailment, but I don't like to be cauterized" (Bukhari).

Al-Baydawi says:

> "The indefinite ["healing" instead of "the healing"] might actually denote emphasis, rather than mean that there is in it some, and not all, healing."

Al-Khazin says:

> Opinions differ. Ibn Masud said, "Honey is a cure for all (outward) diseases, and Quran is a cure for what is (hidden) in the breast." Nafi narrates that if Ibn Umar suffered a wound or any other ailment he would always place honey on the place of the ailment and recite this verse.[17]

Al-Jalalayn writes:

> Honey is good for all things when used with the intention of cure based on this verse, as shown by the hadith of the Prophet (ﷺ)'s order to take honey given

17 Ibn Umar used *ruqya* when there had been scorpion bite.

to the man who had abdominal trouble. (Bukhari and Muslim).

Nawawi says:
Some of the scholars said that the verse is specific, that is, cure is from some diseases and for some people, and the ailment of the man who had abdominal trouble was curable with honey, and they said that the verse did not say that honey was a cure-all . . . It is our way and that of the masses of the Salaf and Khalaf that it is good to (also) resort to medicine as proved by the hadith "For every disease there is a cure," etc.[18]

Qurtubi says:

The Prophet (ﷺ) said, "For every disease there is a cure, and if one takes the right cure for his disease he is cured by Allah's permission."[19] He also said, "O servants of Allah, take medicine (*tadawaw*), for verily Allah did not place (among you) any disease except he placed (among you) a cure for it or a medicine, except one disease and that is death."[20] The scholars are unanimous on the permissibility of using medicine as well as Quranic verses (*istirqa*). Al-Hasan al-Basri hated to use medicine other than made with honey or milk. The Prophet (ﷺ) used Quranic verses for healing the Companions and he ordered them to do the same.

4 *"And We reveal of the Quran what is a healing and a mercy for the believers, and the wrong-doers are not increased except in loss"* (17:82).[21]

5 *"And if I am sick, He heals me"* (26:80).

Qurtubi says:

The expression "I become" attributes authorship of the action to Abraham (ﷺ) out of respect for Allah [i.e. so as not to say Allah makes me become sick], for

18 Commentary on Muslim, *Kitab al-salam* #91, #69.
19 Muslim.
20 Abu Dawud, Tirmidhi (*hasan sahih*).
21 See above, previous section.

sickness and healing is all from Allah. The equivalent
(of such a construction) is the saying of Moses' servant, *"None made me forget it except Satan* (18:63).*"*

Ibn Kathir says:

"Similarly the *jinn* say, *'We do not know if evil is
decreed for those on earth or if their Lord decrees good
for them'* (72:10).[22]

6 *"Say: it (Quran) is a guidance and a healing for those who
believe, and as for disbelievers, their ears are stopped and there
is blindness on them"* (41:44).

Al-Khazin says:

The healing is for what is in the hearts of the sick-
nesses of idolatry and doubt, and it is also said that it
is for ailments and physical illnesses.

Qurtubi says:

Allah makes it known that the Quran, for all who
believe in it, is guidance and healing from doubt and
from physical ailments.

7 *"Nothing ails on the earth and in yourself except it is written in a Manifest Book before We made it to pass"* (57:22).

Qurtubi writes:

Because of this verse, a large group among the
elite (*al-fudala*) relinquished the use of medicine
when sick for the sake of trust and reliance upon
Allah. And they said, "Allah knows the days of sickness and the days of health (in the life of creatures),
and if creatures strive insistently on adding or sub-
tracting from that they cannot."

---

22 Use of the impersonal passive voice with regard to the decreeing of evil.

6.4. Bukhari's Narration of the Hadith on Wearing Protective Verses (*ruqya*) and Remuneration

In Bukhari, *Sahih*, Volume 3, Book 36, Number 476, it is written:

> Narrated Abu Said: Some of the Companions of the Prophet ( ) went on a journey till they reached some of the Arab tribes (at night). They asked the latter to treat them as their guests but they refused. The chief of that tribe was then bitten by a snake (or stung by a scorpion) and they tried their best to cure him but in vain. One of them said, "Nothing has benefited him, will you go to the people who resided here at night, it may be that some of them might have some treatment."
>
> They went to the group of the Companions of the Prophet ( ) and said, "Our chief was bitten by a snake (or stung by a scorpion) and we have tried everything to no avail. Have you got anything that might help?" One of them replied, "Yes, by Allah! I can recite a *ruqya*, but since you have refused to accept us as your guests, I will not recite the *ruqya* for you unless you fix for us some wages for it." They agreed to pay them a flock of sheep. One of them then went and recited (*Surah Fatiha*), "All praise belongs to Allah, the Lord of the Worlds" then breathed over the chief. The latter became all right as if he had been released from a chain, and he got up and started walking, showing no signs of sickness.
>
> They paid them what they agreed to pay. Some of the Companions then suggested to divide their earnings among themselves, but the one who performed the recitation said, "Do not divide them until we go to the Prophet ( ) and narrate the whole story to him, and wait for his order." They went to Allah's Apostle and told him the story. Allah's Apostle said, "How did you come to know that *Surah al-Fatiha* was recited as *ruqya*?" Then he added, "You have done the right thing. Divide what you have earned and assign a

share for me as well." The Prophet (&) smiled thereupon.

Three conclusions can be made based on the above hadith:

1 *Ruqya* carries benefit from one person to another, as suggested in the Prophet's hadith already mentioned, "If you can benefit your brother then do so." *Ruqya* is a benefit, incurred by one sincere person's asking another to come and recite a prayer over an ill person in order to cure him from a sickness. This was done by the Companion who recited over the man who was bitten by a scorpion.
2 The Companion was breathing while performing the *ruqya*. This illustrates that even saliva, which might come out when expelled with the recitation of Holy Quran and Allah's Names and Attributes, will be a cure, as it is known that "The saliva of the believer is a cure."
3 To charge for such a cure, or accept a donation from the person being helped by the *ruqya*, is entirely acceptable, according to the hadith of the Prophet (&) when he said, "Spare me my share," and he was smiling.

6.3.1.THE PROPHET'S SHARE

The above hadith provides clear evidence that whatever good a person owns and whatever good he does—whether in his work, his worship, or anything else pertaining to his acts—the Prophet (&) has a share in it. That is, the Prophet (&) shares in every benefit in our lives. Allah said: *And know that whatever thing you gain, a fifth of it is for Allah and for the Messenger and for the near of kin and the orphans and the needy and the wayfarer, if you believe in Allah and in that which We revealed to Our servant, on the day of distinction, the day on which the two parties met. And Allah has power over all thing.* (8:41).

6.4. A GRAVE MISTRANSLATION IN M. MUHSIN KHAN'S TRANSLATION OF *SAHIH AL-BUKHARI*

M. Muhsin Khan's translation of *Sahih al-Bukhari* contains the following grave error, in Volume 8, Book 76, Number 549:

Narrated Ibn Abbas:

> The Prophet (ﷺ) said, "The people were displayed in front of me and I saw one prophet passing by with a large group of his followers, and another prophet passing by with only a small group of people, and another prophet passing by with only ten (persons), and another prophet passing by with only five (persons), and another prophet passed by alone. And then I looked and saw a large multitude of people, so I asked Gabriel, 'Are these people my followers?' He said, 'No, but look towards the horizon.' I looked and saw a very large multitude of people. Gabriel said, 'Those are your followers, and those are seventy thousand (persons) in front of them who will neither have any reckoning of their accounts nor will receive any punishment.' I asked, 'Why?' He said, 'For they used not to treat themselves with branding (cauterization) nor with *ruqya* (treatment through the recitation of some verses of the Quran) and not to see evil omen in things, and they used to put their trust (only) in their Lord.'" On hearing that, Ukasha bin Mihsan got up and said (to the Prophet (ﷺ)), "Invoke Allah to make me one of them." The Prophet (ﷺ) said, "O Allah, make him one of them." Then another man got up and said (to the Prophet (ﷺ)), "Invoke Allah to make me one of them." The Prophet (ﷺ) said, "Ukasha has preceded you."

As has been abundantly demonstrated in the text of the present section on *tawiz*, there is a pre-Islamic ignorant (*jahili*) meaning for *ruqya*, and there is a traditional (*sunna*), Islamic meaning. The *jahili* meaning is to make a *ruqya* with something that is not allowed in the religion, such as amulets, talismans, spells, incantations, charms, magic and the like. That is what the Prophet (ﷺ) meant in the above hadith, but the translator M. Muhsin Khan has misinterpreted it as the traditional (*sunna*) meaning, which is to use some verses of the Quran or permitted supplications for treatment. Thus he suggests, in his translation, exactly the reverse of what the Prophet (ﷺ) said and practiced, and the reverse of what the Companions said and practiced both in the Prophet's time and after his time. One well-known example, already mentioned, is that one of the Companions used *Surah al-Fatiha* as a *ruqya* to heal a scorpion-bite, and the Prophet (ﷺ) approved of it. Therefore let the reader beware of this unreliable translation in general, as this is but one of many such examples.

The correct translation of the above hadith is:

> The Prophet (ﷺ) said, "The people were displayed in front of me and I saw one Prophet (ﷺ) passing by with a large group of his followers, and another Prophet (ﷺ) passing by with only a small group of people, and another Prophet (ﷺ) passing by with only ten (persons), and another Prophet (ﷺ) passing by with only five (persons), and another Prophet (ﷺ) passed by alone. And then I looked and saw a large multitude of people, so I asked Gabriel, 'Are these people my followers?' He said, 'No, but look towards the horizon.' I looked and saw a very large multitude of people. Gabriel said, 'Those are your followers, and there are seventy thousand of them in front of them who will neither have any reckoning of their accounts nor will receive any punishment.' I asked, 'Why?' He said, 'They used not to treat themselves with cauterization nor amulets, nor to see auguries and omens in birds, and they relied solely upon their Lord.'" On hearing this, Ukkasha ibn Mihsan stood up (*qama ilayhi*) and said to the Prophet (ﷺ), "Invoke Allah to make me one of them." The Prophet (ﷺ) said, "O Allah, make him one of them." Then another man stood up (*qama ilayhi*) and said to the Prophet (ﷺ), "Invoke Allah to make me one of them." The Prophet (ﷺ) said, "Ukkasha has preceded you with this request.

GLOSSARY

ahkam: legal rulings.

ahl al-bida wa al-ahwa: the People of Unwarranted Innovations and Idle Desires.

ahl al-sunna wa al-jamaa: the Sunnis; the People of the Way of the Prophet and the Congregation of Muslims.[1]

aqida pl. *aqa'id*: doctrine.

azaim: strict applications of the law. These are the modes of conduct signifying scrupulous determination to please one's Lord according to the model of the Prophet (ﷺ).

bida: blameworthy innovation.

faqih, pl. *fuqaha*: scholar of *fiqh* or jurisprudence; generally, "person of knowledge."

faqir, pl. *fuqara'*: Sufi, lit. "poor one."

fatwa, pl. *fatawa*: legal opinion.

fiqh: jurisprudence.

fitna: dissension, confusion.

hadith: saying(s) of the Prophet, and the sciences thereof.

hafiz: hadith master, the highest rank of scholarship in hadith.

haqiqi: literal.

hashwiyya: uneducated anthropomorphists.

hijri: adjective from *hijra* applying to dates in the Muslim calendar.

hukm, pl. *ahkam*: legal ruling.

ibadat: worship, acts of worship.

ihsan: perfection of belief and practice.

ijtihad: personal effort of qualified legal reasoning.

isnad: chain of transmission in a hadith or report.

istinbat: derivation (of legal rulings).

jahmi: a follower of Jahm ibn Safwan (d. 128), who said: "Allah is the wind and everything else."[2]

jihad: struggle against disbelief by hand, tongue, and heart.

kalam: theology.

khalaf: "Followers," general name for all Muslims who lived after the first three centuries.

khawarij: "Outsiders," a sect who considered all Muslims who did not follow them, disbelievers. The Prophet said about them as related by Bukhari: "They will transfer the Quranic verses meant to refer to disbelievers and make them refer to believers." Ibn Abidin applied the name of khawarij to the Wahhabi movement.[3]

madhhab, pl. *madhahib*: a legal method or school of law in Islam. The major schools of law include the Hanafi, Maliki, Shafii, and Hanbali and Jafari.

majazi: figurative.

manhaj, minhaj: Way, or doctrinal and juridical method.

muamalat (pl.): plural name embracing all affairs between human beings as opposed to acts of worship *(ibadat)*.

muattila: those who commit *tatil*, i.e. divesting Allah of His attributes.

muhaddith: hadith scholar.

muhkamat: texts conveying firm and unequivocal meaning.

1 See the section entitled "Apostasies and Heresies" in our *Doctrine of Ahl al-Sunna Versus the "Salafi" Movement* p. 60-64.

2 See Bukhari, *Khalq afal al-ibad*, first chapter; Ibn Hajar, *Fath al-bari, Tawhid*, first chapter; and al-Baghdadi, *al-Farq bayn al-firaq*, chapter on the Jahmiyya.

3 al-Sayyid Muhammad Amin Ibn Abidin al-Hanafi, *Radd al-muhtar ala al-durr al-mukhtar, Kitab al-iman, Bab al-bughat* [Answer to the Perplexed: A Commentary on "The Chosen Pearl," Book of Belief, Chapter on Rebels] (Cairo: Dar al-Tibaa al-Misriyya, 1272/1856) 3:309.

mujahid, pl. *mujahidin*: one who wages *jihad*.

mujassima (pl.): those who commit *tajsim*, attributing a body to Allah.

mujtahid: one who practices *ijtihad* or personal effort of qualified legal reasoning.

munafiq: a dissimulator of his disbelief.

mushabbiha (pl.): those who commit *tashbih*, likening Allah to creation.

mushrik, pl. *mushrikun*: one who associate partners to Allah.

mutakallim, pl. *mutakallimun*: expert in *kalam*.

mutashabihat (pl.): texts which admit of some uncertainty with regard to their interpretation.

mutazila: rationalist heresy of the third century.

sahih: sound (applied to the chain of transmission of a hadith).

salaf: the Predecessors, i.e. Muslims of the first three centuries.

salafi: what pertains to the "Salafi" movement, a modern heresy that rejects the principles of mainstream Islam

shafaa: intercession.

sharia: name embracing the principles and application of Islamic law.

suluk: rule of conduct, personal ethics.

tawil: figurative interpretation.

tafwid: committing the meaning to Allah.

tajsim: attributing a body to Allah

tajwid: Quran reading.

takyif: attributing modality to Allah's attributes.

tamthil: giving an example for Allah.

taqlid: following qualified legal reasoning.

tariqa: path, specifically the Sufi path.

tasawwuf: collective name for the schools and sciences of purification of the self.

tashbih: likening Allah to His Creation.

tatil: divesting Allah from His attributes.

tawassul: seeking a means.

tawhid: Islamic doctrine of monotheism.

tazkiyat al-nafs: purification of the self.

usul: principles.

wasila: means.

BIBLIOGRAPHY

Abidin, Ibn, *Hashiyat radd al-muhtar.*
Abidin, Ibn, *Radd al-muhtar ala al-durr al-mukhtar*, 5 vols. (Bulaq 1272/1855). Reprint. Beirut: Dar Ihya' al-Turath al-'Arabi, 1407/1987.
Adani, Ibn Abi Umar al-, *Musnad.*
Adi, Ibn, *al-Kamil fi al-duafa.*
Ahdal, Shaykh Muhammad al-, *Sunniyyat raf al-yadayn fi al-dua bad al-salawat al-maktuba.* Ed. Shaykh Abd al-Fattah Abu Ghudda.
Ahmad, *Kitab al-wara.*
Ahmad, *Musnad.*
Ahmad, *Rawdat al-nazir.*
Ajluni, *Kashf al-khafa.*
Ajurri, *Akhlaq ahl al-quran.* 2nd ed. Ed. Muh. Amr ibn Abd al-Latif (Beirut: dar al-kutub al-ilmiyya, 1407/1987).
Albani, *Daif al-adab al-mufrad.*
Albani, *Sahih al-adab al-mufrad.*
Albani, *Sahih al-Jami al-saghir.*
Albani, *Sahih al-targhib.*
Albani, *Silsila daifa.*
Albani, *Silsila sahiha.*
Allah, Shah Wali, *al-Qawl al-jamil.*
Alwani, Ta Ha Jabir al-, *The Ethics of Disagreement in Islam.*
Amidi, *al-Ihkam fi usul al-ahkam.* 2nd ed. (Beirut, 1401/1982).
Arabi, Ibn al-, *Tuhfat al-ahwadhi.*
Asakir, Ibn, *Tarikh.*
Asfahani, al-Raghib al-, *Mufradat alfaz al-quran.*
Asqalani, Ibn Hajar al-, *Fath al-bari bi sharh Sahih al-Bukhari*, 14 vols. (Cairo: al-Maktaba al-Salafiyya, 1390/1970).
Asqalani, Ibn Hajar, *Tahdhib al-tahdhib* (1993 ed.).
Ata, *Musannaf Ibn Abd al-Razzaq.*
Athir, Ibn al-, *al-Nihaya fi gharib al-hadith wa atharih.*
Athir, Ibn al-, *Jami al-usul fi ahadith al-rasul.*
Awwama, Shaykh Muhammad, *Athar al-hadith al-sharif.*
Ayni, Al-Badr al-, *al-Binaya sharh al-hidaya.*
Azimabadi, Shams al-Haqq, *Awn al-mabud bi sharh sunan abi dawud.*
Baghawi, *Musannaf Abd al-Razzaq.*
Baghawi, *Sharh al-sunna*, 16 vols. (Damascus: al-Maktab al-Islami,

1400/1980).
Baghdadi, *al-Farq bayn al-firaq*.
Baghdadi, *Taqyid al-ilm*.
Barr, Ibn Abd al-, *al-Intiqa*.
Barr, Ibn Abd al-, *al-Istidhkar*.
Barr, Ibn Abd al-, *Jami bayan al-ilm*, (Cairo: dar al-tibaa al-muniriyya).
Bayhaqi, *al-Madkhal*.
Bayhaqi, *Dalail al-nubuwwa*.
Bayhaqi, *Kitab al-adab*.
Bayhaqi, *Shuab al-iman*.
Bazzar, *Musnad*.
Bukhari, *Adab al-mufrad*.
Bukhari, *Khalq afal al-ibad*.
Bukhari, *Sahih al-Bukhari*, 3 vols. Reprint (Beirut: Dar al-Jil, n.d.).
Bukhari, *Sahih al-Bukhari*, 9 vols. (Cairo 1313/1895).
Bukhari, *Tarikh al-saghir*.
Daraqutni, *Sunan*.
Darimi, *Sunan*.
Dawud, Abu, *Manasik*.
Dhahabi, *al-Kabair*.
Dhahabi, *al-Kashshasf fi marifati man lahu riwayatun fi al-kutub al-sitta*.
Dhahabi, *al-Mughni fi al-duafa*.
Dhahabi, *Diwan al-Duafa wa al-matrukin*. Ed. Shaykh Khalil al-Mays. (Beirut: Dar al-fikr, 1408/1988).
Dhahabi, *Lisan al-mizan*.
Dhahabi, *Manaqib Abi Hanifa*.
Dhahabi, *Mizan al-itidal*. ed. Ali Muhammad al-Bajawi (Cairo: al-Halabi).
Dhahabi, *Mujam al-shuyukh al-kabir*.
Dhahabi, *Siyar alam al-nubala*.
Dhahabi, *Tadhhib al-tahdhib* 1st ed. (Hyderabad: Da'irat al-maarif al-nizamiyya, 1327).
Dhahabi, *Tadhkirat al-huffaz*.
Dhahabi, *Tarikh al-Islam*.
Fayruzabadi, *Qamus*.
Ghazali, *Ihya ulum ad-din (Kitab al-adab)*.
Ghudda, Abd al-Fattah Abu, *Radd ala abatil wa iftiraat Nasir al-Albani wa sahibihi sabiqan Zuhayr al-Shawish wa muazirihima*.
Ghudda, Abu, *al-Raf*.
Guillaume, A. trans. *The Life of Muhammad: A Translation of*

Ishaq's Sirat Rasul Allah.
Hajar, Ibn *Fath al-bari* (1989 ed.).
Hajar, Ibn, *al-Isaba.*
Hajar, Ibn, *al-Qawl al-musaddad fi al-dhabb an musnad Ahmad.*
Hajar, Ibn, *Bulugh al-maram.*
Hajar, Ibn, *Fath al-bari bi sharh sahih al-Bukhari* (1989 ed.).
Hajar, Ibn, *Hadi al-Sari.*
Hajar, Ibn, *Nukat.*
Hajar, Ibn, *Tahdhib al-tahdhib.*
Hakim, *al-Tarikh.*
Hakim, *Marifat ulum al-hadith.*
Hakim, *Mustadrak.*
Hanafi, al-Sayyid Muhammad Amin Ibn Abidin al-, *Radd al-muhtar ala al-durr al-mukhtar, Kitab al-Iman, Bab al-bughat* (Cairo: Dar al-Tibaa al-Misriyya, 1272/1856).
Hanafi, Al-Zaylai al-, *Tabyin al-haqaiq: sharh Kanz al-daqaiq.*
Hanafi, Ibn Abidin al-, *Hashiyat radd al-muhtar ala al-durr al-mukhtar.*
Hanbali, *al-Mughni* (1994 ed.).
Hanbali, Ibn Qudama al-, *al-Aqaid.*
Hanifa, Abu, *al-Fiqh al-akbar.*
Harithi, Muhammad Qasim Abduh al-, *Makanat al-Imam Abi Hanifa bayn al-muhaddithin.*
Harun, Yazid ibn, *Khalq afal al-ibad* (1990 ed.).
Hasan, Ahmad, *The Doctrine of Ijma in Islam* (Islamabad: Islamic Research Institute, 1976).
Haskafi, *al-Durr al-mukhtar.*
Hatim, Ibn Abi, *al-Jarh wa al-tadil.*
Haytami, Ibn Hajar al-, *al-Khayrat al-hisan fi manaqib Abi Hanifa al-Numan.*
Haytami, *Majma al-zawaid.*
Hazm, Ibn, *al-Ihkam fi usul al-ahkam.*
Hazm, Ibn, *al-Muhalla.*
Hibban, Ibn, *al-Majruhim min al-muhaddithin wa al-duafa wa al-matrukin,* ed. Mahmud Ibrahim Zayid.
Hibban, Ibn, *Kitab al-majruhin.*
Humam, Ibn al-, *Fath al-qadir.*
Imad, Ibn, *Shadharat al-dhahab.*
Irabi, Ibn al-, *al-Qubal.*
Iraqi, *Mughni an haml al-asfar.*
Islahi, Muhammad Yusuf, *Everyday Fiqh.* Vol. I Trans. Abdul Aziz Kamal (Islamic Publications (Pvt.) Limited: Lahore, Pakistan, c.

1975 - 1993).

Iyad, Qadi, *al-Shifa*.

Jarrahi, *Kashf al-khafa*.

Jassas, *Ahkam al-quran*.

Jawzi, Ibn al-, *al-Mawduat*.

Jawzi, Ibn al-, *Manaqib ashab al-hadith*.

Jaziri, Abd al-Rahman al-, *al-Fiqh ala al-madhahib al-arbaa*.

Jaziri, *al-Fiqh ala al-madhahib al-arbaa*.

Jibali, Muhammad al-, ed. *The Night Prayer / Qiyam and Tarawih*.

Kabbani, Shaykh M. Hisham, trans. *The Doctrine of Ahl al-Sunna Versus the "Salafi" Movement* (As-Sunna Foundation of America, 1996).

Kamali, Mohammad Hashim, *Principles of Islamic Jurisprudence*.

Kasani, *Badai al-sanai*.

Kathir, Ibn, *al-Bidaya wa al-nihaya*.

Kattani, Muhammad ibn afar al-, *al-Risala al-mustatrafa*.

Kawthari, *al-Imta bi sirat al-imamayn al-Hasan ibn Ziyad wa sahibihi Muhammad ibn Shuja*.

Kawthari, *Fiqh ahl al-Iraq*.

Kawthari, *Nasb al-raya*.

Kawthari, *Tanib al-khatib ala ma saqahu fi tarjimat abi hanifa min al-akadhib*.

Khatib, *al-Faqih wa al-mutafaqqih*.

Khatib, *al-Kifaya*.

Khatib, *Tarikh Baghdad*.

Khattabi, *Gharib al-hadith*.

Khazraji, *Khulasat tadhhib tahdhib al-kamal*.

Lucknawi, Abd al-Hayy al-, *Umdat al-riaya fi hall sharh al-wiqaya*.

Lucknawi, *al-Ajwiba al-fadila ala al-asila al-ashra al-kamila*.

Lucknawi, *al-Raf wa al-takmil*.

Main, Ibn, *Tarikh*.

Malik, *Muwatta*.

Maliki, Ibn al-Arabi al-, *Aridat al-ahwadhi*.

Manzhur, Ibn, *Lisan al-Arab*.

Maqdisi, *al-Udda sharh al-umda*.

Marghinani, *al-Hidaya*.

Mawdudi, *Rasail-o-masail*.

Misri, *Umdat al-salik*.

Mizzi, *Tahdhib al-kamal*.

Muflih, Ibn, *al-Adab al-shariyya*.

Muhammad, Sayf al-Din Ahmad ibn, *al-Albani Unveiled*.

Mulaqqin, Ibn al-, *Tuhfat al-muhtaj ila adillat al-Minhaj*.

Munawi, *Sharh al-Jami al-saghir*.
Mundhir, Ibn al-, *al-Awsat*.
Mundhir, Ibn al-, *Kitab al-ijma* (Dar al-dawa in Doha: Qatar, 1401 H).
Mundhiri, *al-Targhib wa al-tarhib*.
Mundhiri, *Mukhtasar al-sunan*.
Muqri', Ibn al-, *al-Rukhsa fi taqbil al-yad* (Riyad ed. 1987).
Muslim, *al-Kuna wa al-asma*.
Muslim, *Kitab al-fadail*.
Muslim, *Sahih Muslim*, 5 vols. Cairo 1376/1956. Reprint. Beirut: Dar al-Fikr, 1403/1983, 1.222: 259.
Nas, Ibn Sayyid al-, *Sharh al-Tirmidhi*.
Nasai, *al-Duafa wa al-matrukin*.
Nasai, *Sunan*.
Nawawi, *al-Majmu*.
Nawawi, *al-Rukhsa bi al-qiyam*.
Nawawi, *al-Tarkhis fi al-ikram bi al-qiyam li dhawi al-fadl wa al-maziyya min ahl al-islam ala jihat al-birr wa al-tawqir wa al-ihtiram la ala jihat al-riya wa al-izam*. Ed. Kilani Muhammad Khalifa (Beirut: Dar al-Basha'ir al-islamiyya, 1409/1988).
Nawawi, *Fatawa*.
Nawawi, *Minhaj al-talibin*.
Nawawi, *Sahih Muslim bi Sharh al-Nawawi*, 18 vols (Cairo 1349/1930). Reprint (18 vols. in 9). Beirut: Dar al-Fikr, 1401/1981.
Nawawi, *Sharh al-muhadhdhab*.
Nawawi, *Sharh Sahih Muslim*.
Nawawi, *Sharh Sahih Muslim.Kitab al-Jihad* (al-Mays ed.).
Nuaym, Abu, *Hilyat al-awliya*.
Qalaji, Muhammad Rawwas, *Mawsuat fiqh Abd Allah ibn Umar* (Beirut: Dar al-nafais, 1986).
Qari, Ali al-, *Mutaqad Abi Hanifa al-Imam fi abaway al-rasul alayhi al-salat wa al-salam*.
Qari, Ali al-, *Sharh al-fiqh al-akbar* (1984 ed.).
Qasimi, Jamal al-Din al-, *Risalat al-jarh wa al-tadil*.
Qayrawani, Ibn Abi Zayd al-, *Jami fi al-sunan* (1982 ed.).
Qayyim, Ibn al-, *Zad al-maad*.
Qayyim, Ibn, *Alam al-muwaqqiin an rabb al-alamin*.
Qayyim, Ibn, *al-Hadi al-nabawi*.
Qayyim, Ibn, *Ilam al-muwaqqiin*.
Qudama, Ibn, *al-Mughni* (1994 ed.).
Qudama, Ibn, *al-Rawda fi usul al-fiqh*.
Qudama, Ibn, *Muqaddimat al-Mughni*.

Qudama, Ibn, *Rawdat an-Nazir.*
Qunfudh, Ibn, *Wasilat al-islam.*
Qurashi, *al-Jawahir al-mudiyya fi manaqib al-hanafiyya.*
Qurtubi, *Jami li ahkam al-quran* (Dar al-hadith ed.).
Qurtubi, *Tafsir.*
Rabi, *Kitab al-umm* (Azhar ed.).
Rushd, Ibn, *Bidayat al-mujtahid.*
Sabiq, Sayyid, *Fiqh al-sunna.*
Sad, Ibn, *Tabaqat.*
Sajzi, Abu al-Nasr al-, *al-Ibana.*
Sakhawi, *al-Jawahir wa al-durar fi tarjamat shaykh al-islam Ibn Hajar*, ed. Hamid Abd al-Majid and Taha al-Zayni (Cairo: wizarat al-awqaf, 1986).
Sakhawi, *al-Jawahir wa al-durar.*
Sakhawi, *al-Maqasid al-hasana.*
Sakhawi, *Fath al-mughith.*
Salah, Ibn, *Muqaddima.*
Sanani, *Raf al-astar li ibtali adillat al-qa'ilina bi fanai al-nar.* Ed. Albani (Beirut & Damascus: al-maktab al-islami, 1405/1984).
Sanani, *Subul al-salam.*
Saqqaf, Hasan Ali al-, *Qamus shata'im al-Albani.*
Saqqaf, Shaykh Hasan al-, *al-Lajif al-dhuaf li al-mutalaib bi ahkam al-itikaf.*
Saqqaf, Shaykh Hasan al-, *Qamus shataim al-Albani.*
Sarakhsi, *al-Mabsut.*
Sawi, Salah al-, *al-Thawabit wa al-mutaghayyirat* (Cairo: al-munta-da al-Islami, 1414 /1994). Trans. Suhail I. Laher
Shafii, Ibrahim ibn Muhammad al-Bajuri al-, *Hashiyat al-bajuri ala sharh ibn al-qasim al-ghazzi ala matn abi shuja.*
Shafii, *Risala.*
Shatibi, *al-Muwafaqat.*
Shatibi, *Kitab al-itisam* (1995 Beirut ed.).
Shawkani, *Irshad al-fuhul.*
Shawkani, *Nayl al-awtar.*
Shayba, Ibn Abi, *Musannaf.*
Shurunbalali, *Nur al-idah wa najat al-qulub.* Trans. Muhammad Abu al-Qasim, *Salvation of the Soul and Islamic Devotions.* (London: Kegan Paul International, 1981).
Subki, Al-Taj al-, *Qaida fi al-jarh wa al-tadil.*
Subki, Al-Taj al-, *Qawaid fi ulum al-hadith.*
Subki, Ibn al-, *Tabaqat al-Shafiiyya.*
Subki, *Qaida fi al-jarh wa al-tadil.*

Subki, *Qawaid fi ulum al-hadith.*
Subki, *Tabaqat al-Shafiiyya.*
Suyuti, *al-Durr al-manthur.*
Suyuti, *Ithaf al-akhissa bi fadail al-masjid al-aqsa.*
Suyuti, *Jazil al-mawahib fi ikhtilaf al-madhahib.*
Suyuti, *Manahil al-safa.*
Suyuti, *Tabyid al-sahifa.*
Tabarani, *Mujam al-kabir.*
Tabari, *Tafsir.*
Tahanawi, *Inja al-watan.*
Tahanawi, Zafar al-, *Qawaid fi ulum al-hadith.* Ed. Abd al-Fattah
  Abu Ghudda.
Tahawi, *Aqida al-tahawiyya.*
Tayalisi, *Musnad.*
Taymiyya, Ibn, *al-Fatawa al-kubra.*
Taymiyya, Ibn, *Aqida wasitiyya.*
Taymiyya, Ibn, *Majmua Fatawa Ibn Taymiyya.*
Taymiyya, Ibn, *Mukhtasar al-fatawa al-misriyya* (Cairo, 1980).
Taymiyya, Ibn, *Naqd maratib al-ijma* (1357 H).
Taymiyya, Ibn, *Qaida fi tawahhud al-milla.*
Taymiyya, Majmu fatawa Ibn Taymiyya.
Tirmidhi, *Kitab al-salat.*
Tirmidhi, *Sunan al-Tirmidhi* 5 vols (Cairo n.d. Reprint. Beirut: Dar
  Ihya al-Turath al-Arabi, n.d.).
Uqayli, *al-Duafa.*
Uqayli, *Kitab al-duafa al-kabir.*
Yala, Abu, *Musnad.*
Yala, Ibn Abi, *Tabaqat al-hanabila.*
Yusuf, Abdur-Rahman ibn, *Fiqhu*l Imaam.
Zabidi, *Ithaf.*
Zabidi, *Taj al-arus.*
Zahra, Abu, *Usul al-fiqh.*
Zarkashi, *Tadhkirah fi al-ahadith al-mushtaharah.*
Zayd, Bakr Abu, *Juz fi mash al-yadayn bad al-dua.*
Zayd, Ibn Abi, *al-Jami fi al-sunan* (1982 ed.).
Zaylai, *Nasb al-raya.*
Zuhayli, *al-Fiqh al-islami wa adillatuh.*

INDEX TO
QURANIC VERSES

INDEX TO HADITH

General Index

ENCYCLOPEDIA OF ISLAMIC DOCTRINE SERIES

VOLUME 1:
ISLAMIC BELIEFS (*AQIDA*)

VOLUME 2:
REMEMBRANCE OF ALLAH AND PRAISING THE PROPHET
(*DHIKR ALLAH, MADIH, NAAT, QASIDAT AL-BURDA*)

VOLUME 3:
THE PROPHET: COMMEMORATIONS, VISITATION
AND HIS KNOWLEDGE OF THE UNSEEN (*MAWLID, ZIYARA,
ILM AL-GHAYB*)

VOLUME 4:
INTERCESSION (*SHAFAA, TAWASSUL, ISTIGHATHA*)

VOLUME 5:
SELF-PURIFICATION: STATE OF EXCELLENCE (*TAZKIYAT AL-
NAFS / TASAWWUF, IHSAN*)

VOLUME 6:
FORGOTTEN ASPECTS OF ISLAMIC WORSHIP: PART ONE

VOLUME 7:
FORGOTTEN ASPECTS OF ISLAMIC WORSHIP: PART TWO

VOLUME 8:
INDICES

AM7202-MP
30